CROCHET PATTERNS

In this book are a collection of crochet patterns, stitches and Amigurumi patterns.

Some patterns are not listed with yarn weight or hook size. I find it best to choose the hook you are more favorable to. Most patterns can be used with a 4.5mm-6.5mm hook, again I find it better to use the hook that you are most comfortable with.

All patterns in this book range from beginner to advanced, but all patterns can be done by a beginner if pattern is followed exactly.

One-hour slippers

Row 1 – ch 3, dc 8 times in 1st st, sl st close.

Row 2 – ch 3, 2 dc in each st around sl st close.

Row 3 – ch 3, {repeat pattern when * * are seen} * dc in 1st st, 2 dc in next stitch * repeat around sl st close.

change color {optional}

row 4 – ch 3, dc in each st around sl st close.

Rows 5 – 7. Repeat row 4.

Row 8 – ch 3, * dc in 1st stitch, 2 dc in next st * repeat around sl st close.

change color {optional}

row 9 – ch 3, dc in each st around sl st close.

Rows 10 – 12 repeat row 9

change color {optional}

row 13 – ch 3, dc next 20, ch 3 turn.

Rows 14 – 20 repeat row 13. Turn inside out, fold flat ends together and sl st together.

****

30-minute beanie

Row 1: Ch-2, dc 8 times in 1st stitch. Join with sl st to top of first dc. (8)

Row 2: Ch-2, 2dc in each st. Join with sl st to top of first dc. (16)

Row 3: Ch-2, *dc in first st, 2dc in next* repeat around. Join with sl st to top of first dc. (24)

Row 4: Ch-2, *d c in first 2 sts, 2dc in next* repeat around. Join with sl st to top of first dc. (32)

Row 5: Ch-2, *dc in first 3 sts, 2dc in next* repeat around. Join with sl st to top of first dc. (40)

Row 6: Ch-2, *dc in first 4 sts, 2dc in next* repeat around. Join with sl st to top of first dc. (48)

Row 7 – 13: Ch-2, dc around. Join with sl st to top of first dc. (48)

if you'd like extra length, continue row 7, adding rows until desired height is reached

Final row: Ch-1, crab stitch around. Join and weave in ends. (48)

****

30 Minute Beginner Crochet Slouchy Hat

Round 1: Ch 2, 8 DC in 1st stitch, sl st to join, Ch 2 (8)

Round 2: 2 Dc in each around, sl st to join, Ch 2 (16)

Round 3: 2 Dc, Dc in next, rep around, sl st to join, Ch 2 (24)

Round 4: 2 Dc, Dc in next 2, rep around, sl st to join, Ch 2 (32)

Round 5-9: Dc in each around, sl st to join, Ch 2 (32)

Round 10: Dc in each around, sl st to join, Ch 1 (32)

Round 11: Sc in each around, sl st to join, Ch 1 (32)

Round 12: Sc in each around, sl st to join, finish off, weave ends (32)

****

Crochet Pineapple Tunic

Front: work in rows

Row 1: Ch 78, dc into 3rd ch from hook, (the first 2 ch doesn't count as 1st dc), skip 2 ch, 2dc − V stitch into next ch, ch3, skip 3ch, sc into next ch, ch6, skip 3ch, sc into next ch, ch3, skip 3ch, 2dc-V stitch into next ch, skip 2ch, dc into next ch,* dc into next ch, skip 2ch, 2dc-V stitch into next ch, ch3, skip 3ch, sc into next ch, ch6, skip 3ch, sc into next ch, ch3, skip 3ch, 2dc- V stitch into next ch, skip 2ch, dc into next ch* repeat ** 3 times.

Row 2: turn, * dc, 2dc-V stitch into next ch2-space, 9 tr into ch6-space, 2dc- V stitch into next ch2-space, dc into next st* repeat ** 4 times.

Row 3: turn, * dc, 2dc- V stitch into next ch2-space, ch2, sc into next st, (ch3, skip 1 st, sc into next st) x 4 times, ch2, 2dc-V stitch into next ch2-space, dc into next st* repeat ** 4 times.

Row 4: turn, * dc, 2dc- V stitch into next ch2-space, ch3, sc into next ch3-space, (ch3, sc into next space) x 3 times, ch3, 2dc-V stitch into next ch2-space, dc into next st* repeat ** 4 times.

Row 5: turn, * dc, 2dc- V stitch into next ch2-space, ch4, sc into next ch3-space, (ch3, sc into next space) x 2 times, ch4, 2dc-V stitch into next ch2-space, dc into next st* repeat ** 4 times.

Row 6: turn, * dc, 2dc- V stitch into next ch2-space, ch5, sc into next ch3-space, ch3, sc into next space, ch5, 2dc-V stitch into next ch2-space, dc into next st* repeat ** 4 times.

Row 7: turn, * dc, 2dc- V stitch into next ch2-space, ch8, sc into ch3-space, ch8, 2dc-V stitch into next ch2-space, dc into next st* repeat ** 4 times.

Row 8: turn, * dc, 2dc-V stitch into next ch2-space, ch3, sc into ch8-space, ch6, sc into next ch8-space, ch3, 2dc- V stitch into next ch2-space, dc into next st * repeat ** 4 times.

Row 9: same as Row 2

Row 10: same as Row 3

Row 11: same as Row 4

Row 12: same as Row 5

Row 13: same as Row 6

Row 14: same as Row 7

Repeat (from Row 8 to Row 14) x 7 more times, until you reach Row 56 (fasten off)

Shoulder part: back to Row 1 of the front.

Row 1: insert hook into the 1st ch of Row 1, dc into 1st ch, skip 2ch, 2dc- V stitch into next ch, ch3, skip 3ch, sc into next ch, ch6, skip 3ch, sc into next ch, ch3, skip 3ch, 2dc- V stitch into next ch, skip 2ch, dc into next ch .Row 2: turn, dc, 2dc- V stitch into next ch2-space, 9 tr into ch6-space, 2dc- V stitch into next ch2-space, dc into last st .

Row 3: turn, dc, 2dc- V stitch into next ch2-space, ch2, sc into next st, (ch3, skip 1 st, sc into next st) x 4 times, ch2, 2dc- V stitch into next ch2-space, dc into last st .

Row 4: turn, dc, 2dc- V stitch into next ch2-space, ch3, sc into next ch3-space, (ch3, sc into next space) x 3 times, ch3, 2dc-V stitch into next ch2-space, dc into last st .

Row 5: turn, dc, 2dc- V stitch into next ch2-space, ch4, sc into next ch3-space, (ch3, sc into next space) x 2 times, ch4, 2dc-V stitch into next ch2-space, dc into last st .

Row 6: turn, dc, 2dc- V stitch into next ch2-space, ch5, sc into next ch3-space, ch3, sc into next space, ch5, 2dc-V stitch into next ch2-space, dc into last st .

Row 7: turn, dc, 2dc- V stitch into next ch2-space, ch8, sc into ch3-space, ch8, 2dc-V stitch into next ch2-space, dc into last st (fasten off, leave long end for seaming)

Repeat at other side to make the other one.

Back: work in rows

From Row 1 to Row 14: same as front part

Repeat (from Row 8 to Row 14) x 8 times until you reach Row 63.

Shoulder part: back to Row 1 of the back.

Row 1: insert hook into the 1st ch of Row 1, dc into 1st ch, skip 2ch, 2dc-

V stitch into next ch, ch3, skip 3ch, sc into next ch, ch6, skip 3ch, sc into next ch, ch3, skip 3ch, 2dc- V stitch into next ch, skip 2ch, dc into next ch

Row 2: turn, dc, 2dc- V stitch into next ch2-space, 9 tr into ch6-space, 2dc- V stitch into next ch2-space, dc into last st (fasten off, leave long end for seaming)

Repeat at other side to make the other one.

From the wrong side, seam shoulder parts with sc or sl (cluster of stitches: dc, 2dc-V stitch) at both sides of the shoulder part.

▪▪▪

Crochet Slippers Pattern

Ch 8 small (ch 10 medium, ch 12 large, ch 14 extra large).

Foundation Round: Sc in 2nd ch from hook, sc in next 5 (7, 9, 11) ch sts, 3 sc in last ch . Do not turn. Rotate work 180 degrees. Sc in bottom loop of next 5 (7, 9, 11) ch sts, 2 sc in bottom loop of last ch st, sl st to beg sc to join round -- 16 (20, 24, 28) sc total.

Row 1: Ch 1 (counts as 1st sc), sc in same st, sc in next 5 (7, 9, 11) sts, 2 sc in next st, sc in next st, 2 sc in next st, sc in next 5 (7, 9, 11) sts, 2 sc in next st, sc in last st, sl st to beg ch to join round -- 20 (24, 28, 32) sc.

Row 2: Ch 1 (counts as 1st sc), sc in same st, sc in next 7 (9, 11, 13) sts, 2 sc in next st, 1 sc in next st, 2 sc in next st, sc in next 7 (9, 11, 13) sts, 2 sc in next st, 1 sc in last st, sl st to beg ch to join round -- 24 (28, 32, 36) sc.

Row 3: Ch 1 (counts as 1st sc), sc in same st, sc in next 9 (11, 13, 15) sts, 2 sc in next st, 1 sc in next st, 2 sc in next st, sc in next 9 (11, 13, 15) sts, 2 sc in next st, 1 sc in last st, sl st to beg ch to join round -- 28 (32, 36, 40) sc.

Row 4: Ch 1 (counts as 1st sc), sc in each st around, sl st to beg ch to end -- 28 (32, 36, 40) sc.

*Repeat Row 4 until piece measures 3 (3.5, 4, 4)'' from toe.

You will now begin working flat in rows.

Row 1: Do not ch . Sc in next 4 (4, 5, 5) sts, turn.

Row 2: Ch 1, sc in next 22 (24, 28, 30) sts, turn.

11

*Repeat Row 2 until foot measures 8.75 (9.75, 10.75, 10.75)" from tip of toe, or 0.25" less than desired foot length.

Row 3: Ch 1, sc in next 15 (16, 19, 20) sts, turn.

Row 4: Ch 1, sc in next 8 (8, 10, 10) sts, turn.

*Repeat Row 4 for 1.25 (1.25, 2, 2)," or until flap is long enough to fold up and meet sides of bootie to close back of foot.

Last Row: Ch 1, sc2tog, sc in next 4 (4, 6, 6) sts, sc2tog -- 6 (6, 8, 8) sc.

Fasten off yarn.

How to Assemble Crochet Slippers

You will now assemble the crochet slippers into the correct shape by closing up the back of the slippers.

Thread tapestry needle with yarn.

Fold heel flap up to close the back of the bootie.

Sew edges of flap in place.

Fasten off yarn.

Slipper Edging

Join yarn to ankle of crochet slipper at center back of heel.

Row 1: Work 60 (66, 72, 74) sc evenly spaced around entire ankle opening as an edging. Use the formula of 4 sts per inch to help you space your sts evenly.

Row 2: Ch 1, sc2tog, sc in every st around to last 2 sts, sc2tog, sl st to beg ch to join -- 58 (64, 70, 72) sc.

Row 3: Ch, sc in every st to end of round, sl st to beg ch to join.

Try on slippers and repeat Round 2 if necessary to get correct fit.

Fasten off yarn and weave in ends.

****

Crocodile crochet stitch

Here are the instructions for one of the most popular ways to crochet crocodile stitch.

Step 1: Crochet a foundation chain that is a multiple of 10 stitches + 1. In this example, I've crocheted a starting chain of 31 stitches.

crochet foundation chain

Step 2: Work 2 dc in 6th chain from hook. This counts as the first set of 1 dc, space, 2 dc.

dc crochet

Step 3: Chain 1. Skip 2 chains. Dc in next stitch.

Step 4: Chain 1. Skip 2 chains. 2 dc in next stitch.

row one crochet

Step 5: Repeat steps 3 and 4 across row. You will end with 2 dc in the last stitch of your foundation row. This will give you a row of 2 dc alternated with 1 dc.

row one crochet

You will now begin the first row of crocodile scale stitches.

Step 6: Chain one and turn.

Step 7: Skip the first dc (which was the last dc of the previous row).

bpdc

Step 8: Work 5 bpdc around the post of the second double crochet in the row. These are worked from the top down, so that the second bpdc is worked around the same post directly below the first bpdc. This makes the first half of the first crocodile scale.

Step 9: Crochet 5 dc post stitches around the next dc post in your row working from bottom to top.

You will insert your hook from the left side to the right (if you are right-handed) and dc around the post. This creates the second half of the first crocodile scale. Step 8 should be a mirror image of Step 7.

Step 10: Slip stitch in the next dc. This secures the crocodile scale to the row.

Step 11: Repeat steps 8-10 across the row. You will end with a scale (so you will not do the last slip st at the very end of the row).

You should notice that you are always working a slip st in the first dc of a pair from the row below, then you work the first half of the crocodile scale in the second dc of the pair and the second half of the crocodile scale in the dc that stands alone in the row below.

You are now ready to create the next set of alternating dc stitches that will look similar to the row that you had at the end of step five.

Step 12: Turn and chain 1.

Step 13: Slip st in center of first scale.

Step 14: Ch 4.

Step 15: 2 dc in the next slip st . (You will notice that there are 2 dc in the row below. One has the texture of the five dc worked around it for half of a crocodile scale. The other has no texture and has a slip st at the top. Work your 2 dc into this slip st .)

Step 16: Ch 1, dc in center of scale.

16

Step 17: Ch 1, 2 dc in next slip st .

Step 18: Repeat steps 16 and 17 across row. End with 2 dc in last stitch.

You are now ready to create your next row of crocodile crochet stitches. Repeat steps 6-18 for pattern.

Variation One

This variation is worked exactly the same as above with one exception. There is a "chain one" space added between the first half of the crocodile scale and the second half. Many people find that this makes it easier to work the second half of the scale (which is worked backwards and so requires a unique angle when working).

Variation Two

The rows of crocodile crochet stitch that I've outlined above are slightly staggered so that the scales don't completely overlap each other. However, it's possible to offset them more fully to create an even "scalier" look. Tamara of Moogly has a good description of this variation. You'll see it is similar to the pattern above but there are two extra rows worked in to create the offset pattern.

Variation Three

It is possible to start a crocodile crochet project with a different foundation chain besides the 10+1. In the aforementioned Moogly post, she describes an option of starting with 5+1. Crochet Spot describes an option for starting with a multiple of 6 + 4.

Another common variation is a foundation chain that has a multiple of 4 + 2, in which case you work the first set of paired dc stitches in side-by-side chains instead of in the same chain. Here's a look at how that variation would work.

Chain a multiple of 4 + 2.

Dc in 4th chain from hook.

Ch 1, skip 1, dc, ch 1, skip 1, dc in next 2 stitches

Repeat last step across row.

Ch 1 and turn.

Skip first dc, work crocodile stitch across row (5 bpdc worked top to bottom, 5 dc around next post worked bottom to top, slip st). Turn.

Sc in center of crocodile st .

Ch 1, 2 dc in slip st, ch 1, dc in center of next crocodile stitch

Repeat last step across row. End with ch 1, 2 dc in last dc. Turn.

Ch 1, crocodile stitch across row starting with first dc (don't skip the first one), end with sc in sc.

Ch 3, dc in sc, ch 1.

Dc in center of next crocodile stitch, ch 1, 2 dc in slip st across row.

Repeat steps 5-13 for pattern.

Variation Four

Crocodile crochet stitch is typically worked with 5 post stitches on each half of the scale, However, it can be worked with a different number of post stitches. For example, you could work 4 or 6 post stitches on each half of the scale. As long as the number is the same on each half, the count doesn't matter. It's a preference thing in terms of how your scales will look.

****

Cross over place mat

1. ch 57, sc in 2nd ch from hook and across.

2. ch 2, dc 1st, sk nxt, dc nxt, go back and dc in sk'd st .

rep row 2 until desired length is achieved.

****

Crown Jewels - 12" Square

Round 1: Ch 4 (first 3 ch count as dc), 15 dc in 4th ch from hook, join with sl st in top of beg ch-3. (16 dc)

Round 2: Beg pc (see above), 2 dc in next dc, *pc (see above) in next dc, 2 dc in next dc, rep from * around, join with sl st in top of beg pc. (8 pc)

Round 3: Ch 3 (counts as dc), dc in same pc as joining sl st, dc in next dc, *2 dc in next st, dc in next st; rep from * around, join with sl st in top of beg ch-3. (36 dc)

Round 4: Ch 3 (counts as dc), dc in same ch as joining sl st, pc in next dc, *2 dc in next dc, pc in next dc; rep from * around, join with sl st in top of beg ch-3. (18 pc)

Round 5: Ch 3 (counts as dc), dc in same ch as joining sl st, 1 dc in each of next 2 st, 2 dc in next st, *1 dc in each of next 2 st, 2 dc in next st; rep from * around, join with sl st in top of beg ch-3. (72 dc)

Round 6: Ch 1, sc in same st, sc in next 3 sts, hdc in next 3 sts, dc in next 2 sts, [1 tr, ch 2, 1 tr] in next st, dc in next 2 sts, hdc in next 3 sts, sc in next 3 sts, *sc in next 4 sts, hdc in next 3 sts, dc in next 2 sts, [1 tr, ch 2, 1 tr] in next st, dc in next 2 sts, hdc in next 3 sts, sc in next 3 next sts; rep from * twice more, join with sl st in first sc. (19 st on each side)

Round 7: Ch 1, sc in same st, sc in next 3 sts, hdc in next 3 sts, dc in next 2 sts, tr in next st, in corner space work [3 tr, ch 3, 3 tr], tr in next st, dc in next 2 sts, hdc in next 3 sts, sc in next 3 sts, *sc in next 4 sts, hdc in next 3 sts, dc in next 2 sts, tr in next st, in corner space work [3 tr, ch 3, 3 tr], tr in next st, dc in next 2 sts, hdc in next 3 sts, sc in next 3 sts; rep from * twice more; join with sl st in first sc. Finish off. (25 st on each side)

Round 8: Attach yarn to any corner space, ch 5 (counts as 1 dtr), work 2 dtr until 1 loop of each remains on hook (3 loops on hook), yarn over and through all 3 loops, ch 5, *work 3 dtr into corner space until 4 loops remain on hook, yarn over and through all 4 loops, ch 5, rep from * once more, work 3 dtr into corner space until 4 loops remain on hook, **sk nxt 5 st, work 3 dtr in next st until 1 loop of each remains on hook, (7 loops on hook) yarn over and through all 7 loops, ch 5, work 3 dtr in same st as last dtr group leaving 4 loops on hook, rep from ** 3 times, sk next 7 st, in corner work [3-dtr group, ch 5, 3-dtr group, ch 5, 3-dtr group, ch 5, 3-dtr group (leaving last 4 loops on hook)], continue pattern around square ending with sl st to top of first dtr group. Finish off.

Round 9. Attach yarn to any ch-5 corner space, in corner work [ch 3, 2 dc ch 2, 3 dc], work 6 dc into each ch-5 space working [3 dc, ch 2, 3 dc] into each corner, continue around, join with sl st to top of beg ch 3.

Round. 10: Ch 1, work 1 sc into each dc and [3 sc, ch 2, 3 sc] into each corner, join with sl st to beg sc. Finish off. Weave in ends.

Easter Day Square

Round 1: Ch 3, 11 dc's in ring. Join to top of beginning ch-3. (12 dc)

Round 2: Ch 3, dc in same st, dc in next st, 2 dc's in next st, ch-2, * (2 dc's in next st, dc in next st, 2 dc's in next st, ch-2) * repeat from * to * twice. Join to top of beginning ch-3 with a sl st . (20 dc)

Round 3: Ch 3, dc in same st, dc in next 3 sts, 2 dc's n next st, ch-3, sk ch-2 sp, * (2 dc's in next st, dc in next 3 sts, 2 dc's in next st, ch-3, sk ch-2 sp) * repeat from * to * twice. Join to top of beginning ch-3 with a sl st . Finish off. (28 dc).

Round 4: Join color B with a sl st in any ch-3 corner, ch 3, 4 dc's in same sp, ch 2, sk first 2 sts, 2 dc's in next st, dc in next st, 2 dc's in next st, sk last 2 sts, ch 2, * (5 dc's in ch-3 sp, ch 2, sk first 2 sts, 2 dc's in next st, dc in next st, 2 dc's in next st, ch 2, sk last 2 sts) * repeat from * to * twice. Join to top of beginning ch-3 with a sl st . (40 dc)

Round 5: Ch 3, dc in same st, dc in next 2 sts, insert stitch marker in the

2nd DC just made, dc in next st, 2 dc's in next st, ch-2, sk ch-2 sp, * (2 dc's in first st, dc in next 3 sts, 2 dc's in last st, ch-2, sk ch-2 sp) * repeat around from * to *. Join to top of beginning ch-3 with a sl st . Finish off. (56 dc)

Round 6: Join color A in marked st with a sl st, remove stitch marker, ch 3, (2 dc, ch 3, 3 dc) in same st, * ch 3, sk 3 sts, sk ch-2 sp, sc in first st, ch 3, sk 2 sts, sc in next st, ch 3, sk 2 sts, sc in last st, ch 3, sk ch-2 sp, sk 3 sts, ** (3 dc, ch 3, 3 dc) in next st . * Repeat from * to * 2 times and from * to ** once. Join to top of beginning ch-3 with a sl st . (24 dc, 12 sc, 20 ch-3 spaces)

Round 7: Sl st to corner, ch 4, (2 tr, ch 3, 3 tr) in same sp, * ch 1, 3 tr in first ch-3 sp, ch 1, (3 dc, ch 1 in next ch-3 sp) repeat once, 3 tr , ch 1 in last ch-3 sp, ** (3 tr, ch 3, 3 tr) in corner sp. * Repeat form * to * 2 times and from * to ** once. Join to top of beginning ch-4 with a sl st . Finish off. (48 tr, 48 dc)

STOP HERE IF YOU WANT AN 8" x 8" SQUARE

Round 8: Join color B in any corner with a sl st, ch 3 (2 dc, ch 3, 3 dc) in corner, * (ch 1, sk 1 st, 3 dc's in center dc, sk 1 st, sk ch–1 sp) repeat 5 times, ch 1, ** (3 dc, ch 3, 3 dc) in corner. * Repeat from * to * 2 times and from * to ** once. Join to top of beginning ch-3 with a sl st . (96 dc)

Round 9: Sl st to corner, ch 3 (2 dc, ch 3, 3 dc) in corner, * (ch 1, sk 1 st, 3 dc's in center dc, sk 1 st) repeat 7 times, ch 1, ** (3 dc, ch 3, 3 dc) in corner. * Repeat from * to * 2 times and from * to ** once. Join to top of beginning ch-3 with a sl st . (120 dc)

STOP HERE IF YOU WANT A 10'' x 10'' SQUARE

Round 10: Sl st to corner, ch 3, (2 dc, ch 3, 3 dc) in corner, * sk 1 st, dc in next 2 sts, ch 1, sk ch–1 sp, dc in next 3 sts, ch 1, (sk ch–1 sp, dc in next 3 sts, ch 1) repeat 7 times, sk ch–1 sp, dc in next 2 sts, sk last st, ** (3 dc, ch 3, 3 dc) in corner. * Repeat from * to * 2 times and from * to ** once. Join to top of beginning ch-2 with a sl st . Finish off. (136 dc)

Round 11: Join color A with a sl st in any corner, ch 1, 3 sc in corner, sc in next st, * (ch 1, sk 1 st or ch–1 sp, sc in next st) repeat across to corner, ** (3 sc in corner). * Repeat from * to * 2 times and from * to ** once. Join to beginning sc. Finish off. (100 sc)

****

Adult Slipper

Ch 50 (women's size 8-10 slipper) (Ch 60 - will make size 10-12 men's slipper)

For smaller foot size, i.e.: 5-7 ch 40.

For larger foot size than 12, add 10 chains to beginning work, i.e.: 13-15 ch 70.

ROW 1: Sc in 2nd ch from hook, sc in each st across, ch 1 and turn

ROW 2 - 12: Sc in each sc across, ch 1, turn.

On the end of Row 12, do not ch 1, just turn. (You can do more rows here for fatter feet) =)

ROW 13: sl st into 1st (13) (17 sts). Ch 1 (counts as a sc) then sc in the next 23 sts (26 sts) - leaving 13 sts (17) unworked. Ch 2 and turn .

ROW 14-15: Dc in the middle stitches, ch 2 and turn

LAST ROW: Alternate 1 fpdc, then 1 bpdc across. End off leaving a long tail of yarn to sew seam.

FINISHING: Fold slipper in half, lengthwise. Stitch down the cuff, across the top of the slipper, down the toe, and across the bottom.

These slippers can be adjusted to fit all sizes and they are really warm!

****

<u>Slipper Pattern</u>

Small (Fits US sizes 5 & 6): Slipper is 9 inches long

Medium (Fits US sizes 7 & 8): Slipper is 9 1/2 inches long

Large(Fits US sizes 9 & 10): Slipper is 10 inches long

Note: Sizes Small and Medium are grouped together and size Large is given separately.

Sizes Small and Medium

Toe Top

1. Work along the free loops of the foundation chain

Round 1: Ch 6, 1 sc in 2nd ch from hook, 1 sc in next 3sts, 4 sc in last st, pivot your work to work along the other side of the foundation chain, 1 sc in next 3 free loops of the foundation ch, 2 sc in last free loop, sl st to first ch . Do not turn.———14 sts

2. Round 2 completed

Note: The end of the round stitch counts include the chains as well.

Round 2: Ch 3, 2 dc in same st as ch 3, ch 1, sk 1, 1 sc in next, *(ch 1, sk 1, 3 dc in next, ch 1, sk 1, 1 sc in next), repeat from * until you end with a sc in the same st as beginning ch-3, ch 1, sl st to the top of beginning ch-3. Do not turn.————24 sts

Note: You will be skipping dc sts to work into the sc.

Round 3: 1 sc in next dc, *(ch 1, 3 dc in next sc, ch 1, 1 sc in the middle dc of the next 3dc group, ch 1, 4 dc in next sc, ch 1, 1 sc in the middle dc of the next 3dc group), repeat from * and after you work 4dc in the last sc st, ch 1, sl st to first sc. Do not turn.————26sts

Round 4: Ch 3, 4 dc in same st as ch-3, ch 1, 1 sc in middle dc of next 3dc group, ch 1, shell in next sc, ch 1, 1 sc in 3rd dc of next 4 dc group, ch 1, shell in next sc, ch 1, 1 sc in middle dc of next 3dc group, ch 1, shell in next sc, ch 1, 1 sc in 3rd dc of next 4 dc group, ch 1, sl st to top of beginning ch 3. Do not turn.————32 sts (4 shells)

Round 5: Sl st into next dc, 1 sc in next, ch 1, shell in next sc, *(ch 1, 1 sc in middle dc of next shell, ch 1, shell in next sc), repeat from * and after shell in the last sc, ch 1, sl st to first sc. Do not turn——32 sts(4 shells)

Round 6: Ch 3, 4 dc in same st as ch-3, *(ch 1, 1 sc in middle dc of next shell, ch 1, shell in next sc), repeat from * and after 1 sc in 3rd dc of the last shell, ch 1, sl st to top of beginning ch 3. Do not turn.————32 sts (4 shells)

Round 7: Repeat Round 5.

Round 8: Repeat Round 6. Do not turn and do not fasten off.

Middle and Back Side of the Slipper

3. Slipper is worked in rows after you complete the toe top

Note: The rest of the slipper is worked in rows and then the back side is seamed to close the slipper.

Row 1: Working in back loops only, ch 2, 1 hdc in same st as ch 2, 1 hdc in next 20 sts, turn.——21 sts

Row 2: Working in front loops only, ch 2, 1 hdc in same st as ch 2, 1 hdc in next 20 sts, turn.——21 sts

4. Measure the length of your slipper

Repeat the above 2 rows until your shoe measures 6 1/2 inches for size Small and 7 inches for size Medium.

Increase Rows

Note: Maintain the sequence of working into the back and front loops. On the right side of the shoe, you will work in back loops and on the wrong side you will work into the front loops.

Increase Row 1: 1 hdc in same st as ch 2, 2 hdc in next, 1 hdc in each st until 2 sts are left, 2 hdc in next, 1 hdc in last st . turn.——23 sts

Repeat the above increase row 2 more times to end in 27 sts and turn.

Next Row: Ch 2, 1 hdc in same st as ch 2, 1 hdc in next 26 sts, turn.——27 sts

5. The last Row completed

Last Row: Ch 1, 1 sc in same st as ch 1, 1 sc in next 3 sts, 1 hdc in next 4 sts, 1 sc in next 2 sts, (sc2tog)3 times, 1 sc in next 2 sts, 1 hdc in next 5 sts, 1 sc in last 4 sts.——24 sts.

6. Sew the back shut with a slip st seam

Now fold and seam the back side of the slipper with sl sts. Fasten off.

Border Around the Slipper

You will now work 2 rounds around the opening of the slipper with a few increases thrown in. This will make your slippers snug and keep it from falling off your feet. You will be working across row ends for the most part and have to distribute your sc as evenly as possible.

7. Work decreases at points shown

Round 1: Sl st to the back seam, ch 1, sc2tog, work sc evenly around the slipper with 5 decreases (sc2tog), 1 at the back, 1 on either side and 1 at each of the corners of the toe top as shown. Sl st to the 1st sc, do not turn. ———-48(52) sts

Round 2: Ch 1, 1 sc in same st as ch 1, *(sk 1 st, 1 sc in next, 1 sc in the previous skipped st), repeat from * to end and sl st to the first sc. Fasten off and weave in the tails.

Your slipper is now ready to keep you warm and comfy!

Size Large

Note: Please take a look at the pictures given for the smaller sizes before you start.

Round 1: Ch 8, 1 sc in 2nd ch from hook, 1 sc in next 5 sts, 4 sc in last st, pivot your work to work along the other side of the foundation chain, 1 sc in next 5 free loops of the foundation ch, 2 sc in last free loop, sl st to first ch . Do not turn.——18 sts

Note: The end of the round stitch counts include the chains as well.

Round 2: Ch 3, 2 dc in same st as ch 3, ch 1, sk 1, 1 sc in next, *(ch 1, sk 1, 3 dc in next, ch 1, sk 1, 1 sc in next), repeat from * until you end with a sc in the same st as beginning ch-3, ch 1, sl st to the top of beginning ch-3. Do not turn.————-30 sts

Note: You will be skipping dc sts to work into the sc.

Round 3: 1 sc in next dc, *(ch 1, 3 dc in next sc, ch 1, 1 sc in the middle dc of the next 3dc group), repeat from * and after you work 3dc in the last sc st, ch 1, sl st to first sc. Do not turn.———-30sts

Round 4: Ch 3, 4 dc in same st as ch-3, *(do not ch 1, 1 sc in middle dc of next 3dc group, ch 1, shell in next sc), repeat from * and after 1 sc in middle dc of last 3 dc group, ch 1, sl st to top of beginning ch 3. Do not turn.————35 sts (5 shells)

Round 5: Sl st into next dc, 1 sc in next, ch 1, shell in next sc, *(do not ch 1, 1 sc in middle dc of next shell, ch 1, shell in next sc), repeat from * and after shell in the last sc, do not ch 1, sl st to first sc. Do not turn——35 sts(5 shells)

Round 6: Ch 3, 4 dc in same st as ch-3, *(do not ch 1, 1 sc in middle dc of next shell, ch 1, shell in next sc), repeat from * and after 1 sc in middle dc of last shell, ch 1, sl st to the top of beginning ch 3. Do not turn.————35 sts (5 shells)

Round 7: Repeat Round 5.

Round 8: Repeat Round 6. Do not turn and do not fasten off.

Middle and Back Side of the Slipper

Note: This part is worked in rows and then the back side is seamed to close the slipper.

Row 1: Working in back loops only, ch 2, 1 hdc in same st as ch 2, 1 hdc in next 22 sts, turn.——23 sts

Row 2: Working in front loops only, ch 2, 1 hdc in same st as ch 2, 1 hdc in next 22 sts, turn.——23 sts

Repeat the above 2 rows until your shoe measures 7 inches.

Increase Rows

Note: Maintain the sequence of working into the back and front loops. On the right side of the shoe, you will work in back loops and on the wrong side you will work into the front loops.

Increase Row 1:1 hdc in same st as ch 2, 2 hdc in next, 1 hdc in each st until 2 sts are left, 2 hdc in next, 1 hdc in last st . turn.——25 sts

Repeat the above increase row 2 more times to end in 29 sts and turn.

Next Row: ch 2 1 hdc in same st as ch 2, 1 hdc in next 26 sts, turn.——29 sts

Repeat above row one more time.

Last Row: Ch 1, 1 sc in same st as ch 1, 1 sc in next 3 sts, 1 hdc in next 5 sts, 1 sc in next 2 sts, (sc2tog)3 times, 1 sc in next 2 sts, 1 hdc in next 6 sts, 1 sc in last 4 sts.——26 sts.

Now fold and seam the back side of the slipper with sl sts. Fasten off.

Border Around the Slipper

You will now work 2 rounds around the opening of the slipper with a few increases thrown in. This will make your slippers snug and keep it from falling off your feet. You will be working across row ends for the most part and have to distribute your sc as evenly as possible.

Round 1: Sl st to the back seam, ch 1, sc2tog, work sc evenly around the slipper with 7 decreases (sc2tog), 1 at the back, 2 on either side and 1 at each of the corners of the toe top as shown (see pic for smaller sizes). Sl st to the 1st sc, do not turn.———-57 sts

Round 2: Ch 1, 1 sc in same st as ch 1, *(sk 1 st, 1 sc in next, 1 sc in the previous skipped st), repeat from * to end and sl st to first sc. Fasten off and weave in the tails.

Your slipper is now ready to keep your feet warm and comfy!

****

Lacy Sun

Round 1: Ch 3, 11 dc in loop, join to 3rd ch of beg ch 3.

Round 2: Ch 1, (sc, ch 3) in each dc around (12 loops), join to 1st sc.

Round 3: Sl st in first loop, beg cluster in loop, ch 3 (cluster in next loop, ch

3) around, join to top of 1st cluster. Finish off CA.

Round 4: Join CB in any ch 3 loop, ch 1, 5 sc in each loop around, join to 1st sc.

Round 5: Sl st in next 2 sc, (ch 4, 2 trc, ch 3, 3 trc) in same st, [*ch 1, skip next 4 sc, 3 dc in next sc, ch 1, skip next 2 sc, 3 hdc in next sc, ch 1, skip next 2 sc, 3 dc in next sc, ch 1, skip 3 sc*, (3 trc, ch 3, 3trc) in next sc] 3 times and * to * once more, join to 4th ch of beg ch 4.

Round 6: Sl st to corner, (ch 3, 2 dc, ch 3, 3 dc) in corner, [*ch 1, (3 dc in next sp, ch 1) 4 times*, (3dc, ch 3, 3 dc) in corner] 3 times and * to * once more, join to 3rd ch of beg ch 3. Finish off CB. This would make a good square on it's own. I believe it would measure about 7 inches.

Round 7: Join CA in any corner, ch 1, [(sc, ch 5, sc) in corner, (ch 5, sc in next sp) 5 times, ch 5] 4 times, join to 1st sc.

Round 8: Sl st in next loop, ch 1, 5 sc in each loop around, join to 1st sc.

Round 9: Sl st in next 2 sc, (ch 3, 2dc, ch 3, 3 dc) in same sc, [*(ch 2, skip 4 sc, 3 dc in next sc) 6 times, ch 2*, (3dc, ch 3, 3dc) in corner sc] 3 times and * to * once more, join to 3rd ch of beg ch 3.

Round 10: Sl st to corner, (ch 3, 2dc, ch 3, 3dc) in corner, [*skip next dc, (V-Stitch in center dc of next 3dc group, dc in next sp) 7 times, V-Stitch in center dc of next 3dc group, skip next dc* (3dc, ch 3, 3dc) in corner] 3 times and * to * once more, join to 3rd ch of beg ch 3.

Round 11: Sl st to corner, ch 2, 4 hdc in corner, [hdc in each st and sp across, 5 hdc in corner] 3 times, hdc in each st and sp across, join to 3rd ch of beg ch 3. Finish off, and weave away.

****

LUSCIOUS LACE CROCHET BLANKET

Note: Afghan is crocheted in multiples of 9 plus 3.

Row 1 (RS): Ch 138, sc in 2nd ch from hook, ch 3, sc in next ch, *skip 3 chs, Fan Shell in next ch, skip 3 chs, sc in next ch, ch 3, sc in next ch, repeat from * across, turn.

Row 2: Ch 3, 2 dc in ch 3 space, ch 2, skip 2 ch 1 spaces, Picot in next ch 1 space, ch 2, *skip 2 ch 1 spaces, Shell in next ch 3 space, ch 2, skip 2 ch

1 spaces, Picot in next ch 1 space, ch 2, repeat from * across to last 3 spaces, skip 2 ch 1 spaces, 2 dc in last ch 3 space, dc in last sc, turn.

Row 3: Ch 1, Picot in first dc, skip ch 2 space, Fan Shell in ch 3 space of Picot, *skip ch 2 space, Picot in ch 2 space of Shell, skip ch 2 space, Fan Shell in ch 3 space of Picot, repeat from * across to last ch 2 space, skip last ch 2 space and 2 dc, Picot in last dc, turn.

Continue pattern repeating Rows 2 and 3 for a total of 77 rows, fasten off

****

Pineapple racerback tank top

Top: (crochet in rounds)

Ch 114, sl into 1st stitch to join.

R1: dc around, 114 sts, sl into 1st stitch to join.

R2: *dc, skip 2 sts, 2dc-V stitch into next st, ch 3, skip 3 sts, sc into next st, ch 6, skip 3 sts, sc into next st, ch 3, skip 3 sts, 2dc-V stitch into next st, skip 2 sts, dc into next st * repeat ** 6 times around, sl into 1st stitch *to join.*

R3: *dc, 2dc-V stitch into next ch2-space, 9 tr into next ch6-space, 2dc-V stitch into next ch2-space, dc into next st* repeat ** 6 times around, sl into 1st stitch to join.

R4: *dc, 2dc-V stitch into next ch2-space, ch 2, sc into next st (the tr of previous round), (ch 3, skip 1 st, sc into next st) x 4 times, ch 2, 2dc-V stitch into next ch2-space, dc into next st* repeat ** 6 times around, sl into 1st stitch to join.

R5: *dc, 2dc-V stitch into next ch2-space, ch 3, sc into next ch3-space, (ch 3, sc into next ch3-space) x 3 times, ch 3, 2dc-V stitch into next ch2-space, dc into next st* repeat ** 6 times around, sl into 1st stitch to join.

R6: *dc, 2dc-V stitch into next ch2-space, ch 4, sc into next ch3-space, (ch 3, sc into next ch3-space) x 2 times, ch 4, 2dc-V stitch into next ch2-space, dc into next st* repeat ** 6 times around, sl into 1st stitch to join.

R7: *dc, 2dc-V stitch into next ch2-space, ch 5, sc into next ch3-space, ch 3, sc into next ch3-space, ch 5, 2dc-V stitch into next ch2-space, dc into next st* repeat ** 6 times around, sl into 1st stitch to join.

R8: *dc, 2dc-V stitch into next ch2-space, ch 8, sc into next ch3-space, ch 8, 2dc-V stitch into next ch2-space, dc into next st* repeat ** 6 times around, sl into 1st stitch to join.

R9: *dc, 2dc-V stitch into next ch2-space, ch 3, sc into next ch8-space, ch 6, sc into next ch8-space, ch 3, 2dc-V stitch into next ch2-space, dc into next st* repeat ** 6 times around, sl into 1st stitch to join.

R10: same as R3.

R11: same as R4

R12: same as R5

R13: same as R6

R14: same as R7

R15: same as R8

R16: same as R9

Repeat (R10 to R16) x 2 times. Until you reach R30

R31: same as R3

R32: ch1, hdc around, sl into 1st stitch to join. (fasten off, weave in end)

Back part and shoulder straps:

Back part:

R1: From the 1st ch of 114 chain, sc around, total 114 sts, sl into 1st stitch to join (fasten off, weave in end)

R2: From the 1st stitch of R1, skip 15 sts, crochet 27 sc across, total 27 sts.

R3: turn, 5 dc across, skip 2 sts, 2dc-V stitch into next st, ch 3, skip 3 sts, sc into next st, ch 6, skip 3 sts, sc into next st, ch 3, skip 3 sts, 2dc-V stitch into next st, skip 2 sts, 5 dc across.

R4: turn, 5 dc across, skip 2 sts, 2dc-V stitch into next ch2-space, 9 tr into next ch6-space, 2dc-V stitch into next ch2-space, 5 dc across.

R5: turn, 5 dc across, 2dc-V stitch into next ch2-space, ch 2, sc into next st, (ch 3, skip 1 st, sc into next st) x 4 times, ch 2, 2dc-V stitch into next ch2-space, 5 dc across.

R6: turn, 5 dc across, 2dc-V stitch into next ch2-space, ch 3, sc into next ch3-space, (ch 3, sc into next ch3-space) x 3 times, ch 3, 2dc-V stitch into next ch2-space, 5 dc across.

R7: turn, 5 dc across, 2dc-V stitch into next ch2-space, ch 4, sc into next ch3-space, (ch 3, sc into next ch3-space) x 2 times, ch 4, 2dc-V stitch into next ch2-space, 5 dc across.

R8: turn, 5 dc across, 2dc-V stitch into next ch2-space, ch 5, sc into next ch3-space, ch 3, sc into next ch3-space, ch 5, 2dc-V stitch into next ch2-space, 5 dc across.

R9: turn, 5 dc across, 2dc-V stitch into next ch2-space, ch 6, sc into next ch3-space, ch 6, 2dc-V stitch into next ch2-space, 5 dc across.

****

Pretty Petals granny square

With Color A, ch 6; join with sl st to form a ring.

Rnd. 1: Ch 1, sc in ring, (ch 3, sc in ring) 7 times, dc in first sc to form last ch-3 sp. (8 ch-3 spaces)

Rnd. 2: Work Beg TCL, ch 4, (work TCL in next ch-3 sp, ch 4) around; join with sl st to top of Beg TCL. Finish off.

Rnd. 3: With Color B, sl st in next ch-3 sp, in same sp work (beg DCL, ch 3, DCL) – beg corner made; ch 2, 3 dc in next ch-3 sp; ch 2; *in next ch-3 sp work (DCL, ch 3, DCL) – corner made; ch 2, 3 dc in next ch-3 sp; ch 2; rep from * twice more; join in top of beg DCL.

Rnd. 4: Sl st in next ch-3 sp, beg corner in same sp; ch 2, 2 dc in next ch-2 sp; dc in next 3 dc, 2 dc in next ch-2 sp; ch 2, *in next corner ch-3 sp work corner; ch 2, 2 dc in next ch-2 sp; dc in next 3 dc, 2 dc in next ch-2 sp; ch 2; rep from * twice more, join in top of beg DCL.

Rnd. 5: Sl st in next ch-3 sp, beg corner in same sp; ch 2, 2 dc in next ch-2 sp; dc in next 7 dc, 2 dc in next ch-2 sp; ch 2, *corner in next corner; ch 2, 2 dc in next ch-2 sp; dc in next 7 dc, 2 dc in next ch-2 sp; ch 2; rep from * twice more, join in top of beg DCL.

Rnd. 6: Sl st in next ch-3 sp, beg corner in same sp; ch 2, 2 dc in next ch-

44

2 sp; dc in next 11 dc, 2 dc in next ch-2 sp; ch 2, *corner in next corner; ch 2, 2 dc in next ch-2 sp; dc in next 11 dc, 2 dc in next ch-2 sp; ch 2; rep from * twice more, join in top of beg DCL.

Rnd. 7: Sl st in next ch-3 sp, beg corner in same sp; ch 2, 2 dc in next ch-2 sp; dc in next 15 dc, 2 dc in next ch-2 sp; ch 2, *corner in next corner; ch 2, 2 dc in next ch-2 sp; dc in next 15 dc, 2 dc in next ch-2 sp; ch 2; rep from * twice more, join in top of beg DCL.

Rnd. 8: Sl st in next ch-3 sp, beg corner in same sp; ch 2, 2 dc in next ch-2 sp; dc in next 19 dc, 2 dc in next ch-2 sp; ch 2, *corner in next corner; ch 2, 2 dc in next ch-2 sp; dc in next 19 dc, 2 dc in next ch-2 sp; ch 2; rep from * twice more, join in top of beg DCL.

Rnd. 9: Ch 3, dc in next DCL; *3 dc in next corner ch-3 sp – dc corner made; dc in next DCL, 2 dc in next ch-2 sp; dc in next 23 dc, 2 dc in next ch-2 sp; dc in next DCL; rep from * twice more; 3 dc in next corner ch-3 sp – dc corner made; dc in next DCL, 2 dc in next ch-2 sp; dc in next 23 dc, 2 dc in next ch-2 sp; join in first dc. Finish off, weave in ends, block.

****

Star Fire granny square

Using color A, ch 4 and join to make a ring or use the Magic Adjustable Ring.

Round 1: Ch 3, 11 dc's in ring. Join to top of beginning ch-3. (12 dc)

Round 2: Ch 3, dc in same st, dc in next st, 2 dc's in next st, ch-2, * (2 dc's in next st, dc in next st, 2 dc's in next st, ch-2) * repeat from * to * twice. Join to top of beginning ch-3 with a sl st . (20 dc)

Round 3: Ch 3, dc in same st, dc in next 3 sts, 2 dc's n next st, ch-3, sk ch-2 sp, * (2 dc's in next st, dc in next 3 sts, 2 dc's in next st, ch-3, sk ch-2 sp) * repeat from * to * twice. Join to top of beginning ch-3 with a sl st . Finish off. (28 dc).

Round 4: Join color B with a sl st in any ch-3 corner, ch 3, 4 dc's in same sp, ch 2, sk first 2 sts, 2 dc's in next st, dc in next st, 2 dc's in next st, sk last 2 sts, ch 2, * (5 dc's in ch-3 sp, ch 2, sk first 2 sts, 2 dc's in next st, dc in next st, 2 dc's in next st, ch 2, sk last 2 sts) * repeat from * to * twice. Join to top of beginning ch-3 with a sl st . (40 dc)

Round 5: Ch 3, dc in same st, dc in next 2 sts, insert stitch marker in the 2nd DC just made, dc in next st, 2 dc's in next st, ch-2, sk ch-2 sp, * (2 dc's in first st, dc in next 3 sts, 2 dc's in last st, ch-2, sk ch-2 sp) * repeat around from * to *. Join to top of beginning ch-3 with a sl st . Finish off. (56 dc)

Round 6: Join color A in marked st with a sl st, remove stitch marker, ch 3, (2 dc, ch 3, 3 dc) in same st, * ch 3, sk 3 sts, sk ch-2 sp, sc in first st, ch 3, sk 2 sts, sc in next st, ch 3, sk 2 sts, sc in last st, ch 3, sk ch-2 sp, sk 3 sts, ** (3 dc, ch 3, 3 dc) in next st . * Repeat from * to * 2 times and from * to ** once. Join to top of beginning ch-3 with a sl st . (24 dc, 12 sc, 20 ch-3 spaces)

Round 7: Sl st to corner, ch 4, (2 tr, ch 3, 3 tr) in same sp, * ch 1, 3 tr in first ch-3 sp, ch 1, (3 dc, ch 1 in next ch-3 sp) repeat once, 3 tr , ch 1 in last ch-3 sp, ** (3 tr, ch 3, 3 tr) in corner sp. * Repeat form * to * 2 times and from * to ** once. Join to top of beginning ch-4 with a sl st . Finish off. (48 tr, 48 dc)

STOP HERE IF YOU WANT AN 8'' x 8'' SQUARE

Round 8: Join color B in any corner with a sl st, ch 3 (2 dc, ch 3, 3 dc) in corner, * (ch 1, sk 1 st, 3 dc's in center dc, sk 1 st, sk ch-1 sp) repeat 5 times, ch 1, ** (3 dc, ch 3, 3 dc) in corner. * Repeat from * to * 2 times and from * to ** once. Join to top of beginning ch-3 with a sl st . (96 dc)

Round 9: Sl st to corner, ch 3 (2 dc, ch 3, 3 dc) in corner, * (ch 1, sk 1 st, 3 dc's in center dc, sk 1 st) repeat 7 times, ch 1, ** (3 dc, ch 3, 3 dc) in corner. * Repeat from * to * 2 times and from * to ** once. Join to top of beginning ch-3 with a sl st . (120 dc)

STOP HERE IF YOU WANT A 10'' x 10'' SQUARE

Round 10: Sl st to corner, ch 3, (2 dc, ch 3, 3 dc) in corner, * sk 1 st, dc in next 2 sts, ch 1, sk ch-1 sp, dc in next 3 sts, ch 1, (sk ch-1 sp, dc in next 3 sts, ch 1) repeat 7 times, sk ch-1 sp, dc in next 2 sts, sk last st, ** (3 dc, ch 3, 3 dc) in corner. * Repeat from * to * 2 times and from * to ** once. Join to top of beginning ch-2 with a sl st . Finish off. (136 dc)

Round 11: Join color A with a sl st in any corner, ch 1, 3 sc in corner, sc in next st, * (ch 1, sk 1 st or ch-1 sp, sc in next st) repeat across to corner, ** (3 sc in corner). * Repeat from * to * 2 times and from * to ** once. Join to beginning sc. Finish off. (100 sc)

****

<u>Summer Air Tunic</u>

Back:

R1: ch 117, dc into 3rd ch from hook (first 2 ch doesn't count as 1st dc), 115 dc across, turn.

R2: *dc, skip 2 sts, 2dc-V stitch into next st, skip 2 sts, dc into next st, ch2, skip 2 sts* repeat ** 12 times across, dc into next st, skip 2 sts, 2dc-V stitch into next st, skip 2 sts, dc into last st, turn.

R3: *dc, skip 2 sts, 2dc-V stitch into next ch1-space, skip 2 sts, dc into next st, ch 2, skip next ch2-space* repeat ** 12 times across, dc into next st, skip 2 sts, 2dc-V stitch into next ch1-space, skip 2 sts, dc into last st, turn.

R4 to R58: same as R3

R59: *dc, skip 2 sts, 2dc-V stitch into next ch1-space, skip 2 sts, dc into next st, ch 2, skip next ch2-space* repeat ** 4 times across, dc into next st, turn.

R60: *dc, ch2, skip next ch2-space, dc into next st, skip 2 sts, 2dc-V stitch into next ch1-space, skip 2 sts* repeat ** 4 times across, dc into last st . (fasten off, leave long end for shoulder seaming)

Repeat R59 and R60 at the other side.

Front:

R1: ch 117, dc into 3rd ch from hook (first 2 ch doesn't count as 1st dc), 115 dc across, turn.

R2: *dc, skip 2 sts, 2dc-V stitch into next st, skip 2 sts, dc into next st, ch2, skip 2 sts* repeat ** 12 times across, dc into next st, skip 2 sts, 2dc-V stitch into next st, skip 2 sts, dc into last st, turn.

R3: *dc, skip 2 sts, 2dc-V stitch into next ch1-space, skip 2 sts, dc into next st, ch 2, skip next ch2-space* repeat ** 12 times across, dc into next st, skip 2 sts, 2dc-V stitch into next ch1-space, skip 2 sts, dc into last st, turn.

R4 to R55: same as R3

R56: *dc, skip 2 sts, 2dc-V stitch into next ch1-space, skip 2 sts, dc into next st, ch 2, skip next ch2-space* repeat ** 4 times across, dc into next st, turn.

R57: *dc, ch2, skip next ch2-space, dc into next st, skip 2 sts, 2dc-V stitch into next ch1-space, skip 2 sts* repeat ** 4 times across, dc into last st, turn.

R58: *dc, skip 2 sts, 2dc-V stitch into next ch1-space, skip 2 sts, dc into next st, ch 2, skip next ch2-space* repeat ** 4 times across, dc into last st, turn.

R59: same as R57

R60: same as R58 (fasten off, leave long end for shoulder seaming)

Repeat R56 and R60 at the other side.

Seam shoulder lines with sc.

Seam body lines with sc. (leave 18 rows from the top down for armholes, *leave 12 to 15 rows for side slits)*

****

SUMMER DIAMONDS KIMONO CARDIGAN

BODY:

Row 0: Ch 197. Turn.

Row 1: Ch 2. Starting from 3rd chain from hook, work 1 dc in each of next 6 st . Work [Ch 1, skip 1 st . Work 1 dc in next st . Ch 1, skip 1 st . Work 1 dc in each of next 11 st .] 13 times. Ch 1, skip 1 st . Work 1 dc in next st . Ch 1, skip 1 st . Work 1 dc in each of next 6 st . Turn. (197)

Row 2: Ch 2. Work 1 dc in each of next 5 st . Work [Ch 1, skip 1 st . Work 1 dc in each of next 3 st . Ch 1, skip 1 st . Work 1 dc in each of next 9 st .] 13 times. Ch 1, skip 1 st . Work 1 dc in each of next 3 st . Ch 1, skip 1 st . Work 1 dc in each of next 5 st . Turn. (197)

Row 3: Ch 2. Work 1 dc in each of next 4 st . Work [Ch 1, skip 1 st . Work 1 dc in each of next 5 st . Ch 1, skip 1 st . Work 1 dc in each of next 7 st .] 13 times. Ch 1, skip 1 st . Work 1 dc in each of next 5 st . Ch 1, skip 1 st .

Work 1 dc in each of next 4 st . Turn. (197)

Row 4: Ch 2. Work 1 dc in each of next 3 st . Work [Ch 1, skip 1 st . Work 1 dc in each of next 7 st . Ch 1, skip 1 st . Work 1 dc in each of next 5 st .] 13 times. Ch 1, skip 1 st . Work 1 dc in each of next 7 st . Ch 1, skip 1 st . Work 1 dc in each of next 3 st . Turn. (197)

Row 5: Ch 2. Work 1 dc in each of next 2 st . Work [Ch 1, skip 1 st . Work 1 dc in each of next 9 st . Ch 1, skip 1 st . Work 1 dc in each of next 3 st .] 13 times. Ch 1, skip 1 st . Work 1 dc in each of next 9 st . Ch 1, skip 1 st . Work 1 dc in each of next 2 st . Turn. (197)

Row 6: Ch 2. Work 1 dc in next st. Work [Ch 1, skip 1 st. Work 1 dc in each of next 11 st. Ch 1, skip 1 st. Work 1 dc in next st.] 13 times. Ch 1, skip 1 st. Work 1 dc in each of next 11 st. Ch 1, skip 1 st. Work 1 dc in next st. Turn. (197)

Row 7: Ch 2. Work 1 dc in each of next 2 st. Work [Ch 1, skip 1 st. Work 1 dc in each of next 9 st. Ch 1, skip 1 st. Work 1 dc in each of next 3 st.] 13 times. Ch 1, skip 1 st. Work 1 dc in each of next 9 st. Ch 1, skip 1 st. Work 1 dc in each of next 2 st. Turn. (197)

Row 8: Ch 2. Work 1 dc in each of next 3 st. Work [Ch 1, skip 1 st. Work 1 dc in each of next 7 st. Ch 1, skip 1 st. Work 1 dc in each of next 5 st.] 13 times. Ch 1, skip 1 st. Work 1 dc in each of next 7 st. Ch 1, skip 1 st. Work 1 dc in each of next 3 st. Turn. (197)

Row 9: Ch 2. Work 1 dc in each of next 4 st. Work [Ch 1, skip 1 st. Work 1 dc in each of next 5 st. Ch 1, skip 1 st. Work 1 dc in each of next 7 st.] 13 times. Ch 1, skip 1 st. Work 1 dc in each of next 5 st. Ch 1, skip 1 st. Work 1 dc in each of next 4 st. Turn. (197)

Row 10: Ch 2. Work 1 dc in each of next 5 st. Work [Ch 1, skip 1 st. Work 1 dc in each of next 3 st. Ch 1, skip 1 st. Work 1 dc in each of next 9 st.] 13 times. Ch 1, skip 1 st. Work 1 dc in each of next 3 st. Ch 1, skip 1 st. Work 1 dc in each of next 5 st. Turn. (197)

Rows 11-20: Repeat Rows 1-10.

Row 21-23: Repeat Rows 1-3.

Row 24: Ch 2. Work 1 dc in each of next 3 st. Work [Ch 1, skip 1 st. Work 1 dc in each of next 7 st. Ch 1, skip 1 st. Work 1 dc in each of next 5 st.] 6 times. Ch 1, skip 1 st. Work 1 dc in each of next 7 st. Ch 1, skip 1 st. Work

1 dc in each of next 2 st. Turn. (98)

Row 25: Ch 2. Work 1 dc in next st. Work [Ch 1, skip 1 st. Work 1 dc in each of next 9 st. Ch 1, skip 1 st. Work 1 dc in each of next 3 st.] 6 times. Ch 1, skip 1 st. Work 1 dc in each of next 9 st. Ch 1, skip 1 st. Work 1 dc in each of next 2 st. Turn. (98)

Row 26: Ch 2. Work 1 dc in next st. Work [Ch 1, skip 1 st. Work 1 dc in each of next 11 st. Ch 1, skip 1 st. Work 1 dc in next st.] 6 times. Ch 1, skip 1 st. Work 1 dc in each of next 12 st. Turn. (98)

Row 27: Ch 2. Work 1 dc in next st. Work [Ch 1, skip 1 st. Work 1 dc in each of next 9 st. Ch 1, skip 1 st. Work 1 dc in each of next 3 st.] 6 times. Ch 1, skip 1 st. Work 1 dc in each of next 9 st. Ch 1, skip 1 st. Work 1 dc in each of next 2 st. Turn. (98)

Row 28: Ch 2. Work 1 dc in each of next 3 st. Work [Ch 1, skip 1 st. Work 1 dc in each of next 7 st. Ch 1, skip 1 st. Work 1 dc in each of next 5 st.] 6 times. Ch 1, skip 1 st. Work 1 dc in each of next 7 st. Ch 1, skip 1 st. Work 1 dc in each of next 2 st. Turn. (98)

Row 29: Ch 2. Work 1 dc in each of next 3 st. Work [Ch 1, skip 1 st. Work

1 dc in each of next 5 st. Ch 1, skip 1 st. Work 1 dc in each of next 7 st.] 6 times. Ch 1, skip 1 st. Work 1 dc in each of next 5 st. Ch 1, skip 1 st. Work 1 dc in each of next 4 st. Turn. (98)

Row 30: Ch 2. Work 1 dc in each of next 5 st. Work [Ch 1, skip 1 st. Work 1 dc in each of next 3 st. Ch 1, skip 1 st. Work 1 dc in each of next 9 st.] 6 times. Ch 1, skip 1 st. Work 1 dc in each of next 3 st. Ch 1, skip 1 st. Work 1 dc in each of next 4 st. Turn. (98)

Row 31: Ch 2. Work 1 dc in each of next 5 st. Work [Ch 1, skip 1 st. Work 1 dc in next st. Ch 1, skip 1 st. Work 1 dc in each of next 11 st.] 6 times. Ch 1, skip 1 st. Work 1 dc in next st. Ch 1, skip 1 st. Work 1 dc in each of next 6 st. Turn. (98)

Row 32: Ch 2. Work 1 dc in each of next 5 st. Work [Ch 1, skip 1 st. Work 1 dc in each of next 3 st. Ch 1, skip 1 st. Work 1 dc in each of next 9 st.] 6 times. Ch 1, skip 1 st. Work 1 dc in each of next 3 st. Ch 1, skip 1 st. Work 1 dc in each of next 4 st. Turn. (98)

Row 33: Ch 2. Work 1 dc in each of next 3 st. Work [Ch 1, skip 1 st. Work 1 dc in each of next 5 st. Ch 1, skip 1 st. Work 1 dc in each of next 7 st.] 6

times. Ch 1, skip 1 st. Work 1 dc in each of next 5 st. Ch 1, skip 1 st. Work 1 dc in each of next 4 st. Turn. (98)

Rows 34-37: Repeat Rows 24-27.

Row 38: Ch 2. Work 1 dc in each of next 3 st. Work [Ch 1, skip 1 st. Work 1 dc in each of next 7 st. Ch 1, skip 1 st. Work 1 dc in each of next 5 st.] 6 times. Ch 1, skip 1 st. Work 1 dc in each of next 7 st. Ch 1, skip 1 st. Work 1 dc in each of next 2 st. Ch 99. Turn.

Creating the next flap

Row 39: Ch 2. Work 1 dc in each of next 4 st. Work [Ch 1, skip 1 st. Work 1 dc in each of next 5 st. Ch 1, skip 1 st. Work 1 dc in each of next 7 st.] 6 times. Ch 1, skip 1 st. Work 1 dc in each of next 5 st. Ch 1, skip 1 st. Work 1 dc in each of next 7 st. (Join to the main body after the 4th dc). Work [Ch 1, skip 1 st. Work 1 dc in each of next 5 st. Ch 1, skip 1 st. Work 1 dc in each of next 7 st.] 6 times. Ch 1, skip 1 st. Work 1 dc in each of next 5 st. Ch 1, skip 1 st. Work 1 dc in each of next 4 st. Turn. (197)

Row 40: Ch 2. Work 1 dc in each of next 5 st. Work [Ch 1, skip 1 st. Work 1 dc in each of next 3 st. Ch 1, skip 1 st. Work 1 dc in each of next 9 st.]

13 times. Ch 1, skip 1 st. Work 1 dc in each of next 3 st. Ch 1, skip 1 st. Work 1 dc in each of next 5 st. Turn. (197)

Rows 41-60: Repeat Rows 1-10.

Row 61: Work 1 dc in each stitch across.

Fold the flap down to the line up with the body in order to work the seam. Working through all 4 loops of the double crochet stitches (from Row 61), work 1 sl st in each of next 63 stitches.

Joining seams

For the 64th stitch and onwards, work only on one side of the seam (do not join the seam together). This is the beginning of your sleeve.

Arm Swatch

RIGHT SLEEVE:

Row 1: Insert hook into the 64th stitch, draw up a loop, Ch 2. Work 1 dc in same stitch, 1 dc in next stitch. Work [Ch 1, skip 1 st. Work 1 dc in each of next 9 st. Ch 1, skip 1 st. Work 1 dc in each of next 3 st.] 4 times. Ch 1, skip 1 st. Work 1 dc in each of next 9 st. Ch 1, skip 1 st. Work 1 dc in each of next 2 st. Turn. (71)

Row 2: Ch 2. Work 1 dc in each of next 3 st. Work [Ch 1, skip 1 st. Work 1 dc in each of next 7 st. Ch 1, skip 1 st. Work 1 dc in each of next 5 st.] 4 times. Ch 1, skip 1 st. Work 1 dc in each of next 7 st. Ch 1, skip 1 st. Work 1 dc in each of next 3 st. Turn. (71)

Row 3: Ch 2. Work 1 dc in each of next 4 st. Work [Ch 1, skip 1 st. Work 1 dc in each of next 5 st. Ch 1, skip 1 st. Work 1 dc in each of next 7 st.] 4 times. Ch 1, skip 1 st. Work 1 dc in each of next 5 st. Ch 1, skip 1 st. Work 1 dc in each of next 4 st. Turn. (71)

Row 4: Ch 2. Work 1 dc in each of next 5 st. Work [Ch 1, skip 1 st. Work 1 dc in each of next 3 st. Ch 1, skip 1 st. Work 1 dc in each of next 9 st.] 4 times. Ch 1, skip 1 st. Work 1 dc in each of next 3 st. Ch 1, skip 1 st. Work 1 dc in each of next 5 st. Turn. (71)

Row 5: Ch 2. Work 1 dc in each of next 6 st. Work [Ch 1, skip 1 st. Work 1 dc in next st. Ch 1, skip 1 st. Work 1 dc in each of next 11 st.] 4 times. Ch 1, skip 1 st. Work 1 dc in next st. Ch 1, skip 1 st. Work 1 dc in each of next 6 st. Turn. (71)

Row 6: Ch 2. Work 1 dc in each of next 5 st. Work [Ch 1, skip 1 st. Work 1 dc in each of next 3 st. Ch 1, skip 1 st. Work 1 dc in each of next 9 st.] 4 times. Ch 1, skip 1 st. Work 1 dc in each of next 3 st. Ch 1, skip 1 st. Work 1 dc in each of next 5 st. Turn. (71)

Row 7: Ch 2. Work 1 dc in each of next 4 st. Work [Ch 1, skip 1 st. Work 1 dc in each of next 5 st. Ch 1, skip 1 st. Work 1 dc in each of next 7 st.] 4 times. Ch 1, skip 1 st. Work 1 dc in each of next 5 st. Ch 1, skip 1 st. Work 1 dc in each of next 4 st. Turn. (71)

Row 8: Ch 2. Work 1 dc in each of next 3 st. Work [Ch 1, skip 1 st. Work 1 dc in each of next 7 st. Ch 1, skip 1 st. Work 1 dc in each of next 5 st.] 4 times. Ch 1, skip 1 st. Work 1 dc in each of next 7 st. Ch 1, skip 1 st. Work 1 dc in each of next 3 st. Turn. (71)

Row 9: Ch 2. Work 1 dc in each of next 2 st. Work [Ch 1, skip 1 st. Work 1 dc in each of next 9 st. Ch 1, skip 1 st. Work 1 dc in each of next 3 st.] 4 times. Ch 1, skip 1 st. Work 1 dc in each of next 9 st. Ch 1, skip 1 st. Work 1 dc in each of next 2 st. Turn. (71)

Row 10: Ch 2. Work 1 dc in next st. Work [Ch 1, skip 1 st. Work 1 dc in each of next 11 st. Ch 1, skip 1 st. Work 1 dc in each of next 1 st.] 4 times. Ch 1, skip 1 st. Work 1 dc in each of next 11 st. Ch 1, skip 1 st. Work 1 dc in next st. Turn. (71)

Row 11: Ch 2. Work 1 dc in each of next 2 st. Work [Ch 1, skip 1 st. Work 1 dc in each of next 9 st. Ch 1, skip 1 st. Work 1 dc in each of next 3 st.] 4 times. Ch 1, skip 1 st. Work 1 dc in each of next 9 st. Ch 1, skip 1 st. Work 1 dc in each of next 2 st. Turn. (71)

Row 12: Ch 2. Work 1 dc in each of next 3 st. Work [Ch 1, skip 1 st. Work 1 dc in each of next 7 st. Ch 1, skip 1 st. Work 1 dc in each of next 5 st.] 4 times. Ch 1, skip 1 st. Work 1 dc in each of next 7 st. Ch 1, skip 1 st. Work 1 dc in each of next 3 st. Turn. (71)

Cut a long tail for working the seam. Fasten a knot to secure the last stitch, then use the tail to sew the seam together, ending at the armpit. Fasten off, and weave in ends.

LEFT SEAM:

Working through all 4 loops of the double crochet stitches (from Row 61), work 1 sl st in each of next 63 stitches.

For the 64th stitch and onwards, work only on one side of the seam (do not join the seam together). This is the beginning of your sleeve.

LEFT SLEEVE:

Row 1: Ch 2. Work 1 dc in each of next 3 st. Work [Ch 1, skip 1 st. Work 1 dc in each of next 7 st. Ch 1, skip 1 st. Work 1 dc in each of next 5 st.] 4 times. Ch 1, skip 1 st. Work 1 dc in each of next 7 st. Ch 1, skip 1 st. Work 1 dc in each of next 3 st. Turn. (71)

Row 2: Ch 2. Work 1 dc in each of next 4 st. Work [Ch 1, skip 1 st. Work 1 dc in each of next 5 st. Ch 1, skip 1 st. Work 1 dc in each of next 7 st.] 4 times. Ch 1, skip 1 st. Work 1 dc in each of next 5 st. Ch 1, skip 1 st. Work 1 dc in each of next 4 st. Turn. (71)

Row 3: Ch 2. Work 1 dc in each of next 5 st. Work [Ch 1, skip 1 st. Work 1 dc in each of next 3 st. Ch 1, skip 1 st. Work 1 dc in each of next 9 st.] 4 times. Ch 1, skip 1 st. Work 1 dc in each of next 3 st. Ch 1, skip 1 st. Work 1 dc in each of next 5 st. Turn. (71)

Row 4: Ch 2. Work 1 dc in each of next 6 st. Work [Ch 1, skip 1 st. Work 1 dc in next st. Ch 1, skip 1 st. Work 1 dc in each of next 11 st.] 4 times. Ch 1, skip 1 st. Work 1 dc in next st. Ch 1, skip 1 st. Work 1 dc in each of next 6 st. Turn. (71)

Row 5: Ch 2. Work 1 dc in each of next 5 st. Work [Ch 1, skip 1 st. Work 1 dc in each of next 3 st. Ch 1, skip 1 st. Work 1 dc in each of next 9 st.] 4 times. Ch 1, skip 1 st. Work 1 dc in each of next 3 st. Ch 1, skip 1 st. Work 1 dc in each of next 5 st. Turn. (71)

Row 6: Ch 2. Work 1 dc in each of next 4 st. Work [Ch 1, skip 1 st. Work 1 dc in each of next 5 st. Ch 1, skip 1 st. Work 1 dc in each of next 7 st.] 4 times. Ch 1, skip 1 st. Work 1 dc in each of next 5 st. Ch 1, skip 1 st. Work 1 dc in each of next 4 st. Turn. (71)

Row 7: Ch 2. Work 1 dc in each of next 3 st. Work [Ch 1, skip 1 st. Work 1 dc in each of next 7 st. Ch 1, skip 1 st. Work 1 dc in each of next 5 st.] 4 times. Ch 1, skip 1 st. Work 1 dc in each of next 7 st. Ch 1, skip 1 st. Work 1 dc in each of next 3 st. Turn. (71)

Row 8: Ch 2. Work 1 dc in each of next 2 st. Work [Ch 1, skip 1 st. Work 1 dc in each of next 9 st. Ch 1, skip 1 st. Work 1 dc in each of next 3 st.] 4 times. Ch 1, skip 1 st. Work 1 dc in each of next 9 st. Ch 1, skip 1 st. Work 1 dc in each of next 2 st. Turn. (71)

Row 9: Ch 2. Work 1 dc in next st. Work [Ch 1, skip 1 st. Work 1 dc in each of next 11 st. Ch 1, skip 1 st. Work 1 dc in each of next 1 st.] 4 times. Ch 1, skip 1 st. Work 1 dc in each of next 11 st. Ch 1, skip 1 st. Work 1 dc in next st. Turn. (71)

Row 10: Ch 2. Work 1 dc in each of next 2 st. Work [Ch 1, skip 1 st. Work 1 dc in each of next 9 st. Ch 1, skip 1 st. Work 1 dc in each of next 3 st.] 4 times. Ch 1, skip 1 st. Work 1 dc in each of next 9 st. Ch 1, skip 1 st. Work 1 dc in each of next 2 st. Turn. (71)

Row 11: Ch 2. Work 1 dc in each of next 3 st. Work [Ch 1, skip 1 st. Work 1 dc in each of next 7 st. Ch 1, skip 1 st. Work 1 dc in each of next 5 st.] 4 times. Ch 1, skip 1 st. Work 1 dc in each of next 7 st. Ch 1, skip 1 st. Work 1 dc in each of next 3 st. Turn. (71)

Row 12: Ch 2. Work 1 dc in each of next 4 st. Work [Ch 1, skip 1 st. Work 1 dc in each of next 5 st. Ch 1, skip 1 st. Work 1 dc in each of next 7 st.] 4

times. Ch 1, skip 1 st. Work 1 dc in each of next 5 st. Ch 1, skip 1 st. Work 1 dc in each of next 4 st. Turn. (71)

Cut a long tail for working the seam. Fasten a knot to secure the last stitch, then use the tail to sew the seam together, ending at the armpit. Fasten off, and weave in ends.

SLEEVE TRIM:

Row 1: Work 6 foundation half double crochet stitch. Turn.

Row 2: Ch 2. Starting from 3rd chain from hook, work 1 hdc in each stitch across, back loops only.

Rows 3-44: Repeat Row 2, 42 times, for a total of 44 rows. Join the first and last hdc row by working 6 sl st across.

Fasten off, leaving a long tail. Use the tail to join the trim evenly to the sleeve using a mattress stitch. Fasten off and weave in ends.

BOTTOM TRIM:

Row 1: Work 6 foundation hdc stitches. Turn.

Row 2: Ch 2. Starting from 3rd chain from hook, work 1 hdc in each stitch across, back loops only.

Rows 3-145: Repeat Row 2, 143 times, for a total of 145 rows.

Fasten off, leaving a long tail. Use the tail to join the trim evenly to the body's bottom border using a mattress stitch. Fasten off and weave in ends.

COLLAR TRIM:

Row 1: Work 8 foundation hdc stitches. Turn.

Row 2: Ch 2. Starting from 4rd chain from hook, work 1 hdc in each stitch across, back loops only.

Rows 3-178: Repeat Row 2, 176 times, for a total of 178 rows.

Fasten off, leaving a long tail. Use the tail to join the trim evenly to the body's collar (up one side, across the back, down the other side) using a mattress stitch. Fasten off and weave in ends.

■■

Winter Dream

ch 4

Round 1: (dc, ch 1) in 4th ch from hook, (2 dc, ch 1) 7 times in same st, join with sl st in top of beg ch . (16 dc, 8 ch 1 sps)

Round 2: sl st in next dc, sl st in next ch 1 sp, ch 1, (sc, dc, ch 1, dc, sc) in same ch 1 space, (sc, dc, ch 1, dc, sc) in next ch 1 space 7 times, join with sl st in top of beg sc. (8 petals)

Round 3: sl st in next dc, sl st in next ch 1 sp, ch 1, sc in same space, ch 3, (sk next 4 sts, sc in next ch 1 sp, ch 3) 7 times, join with sl st in top of beg sc. (8 ch 3 sps)

Round 4: ch 4 (counts as beg ch 3 + ch 1), dc in same space, 5 dc in next ch 3 space, dc in next sc, 5 dc in next ch 3 space, *(dc, ch 1, dc) in next sc, 5 dc in next ch 3 space, dc in next sc, 5 dc in next ch 3 space, rep from * twice more, join with sl st in top of beg ch 3. (52 dc, 4 ch 1 sps)

Round 5: ch 3, *(2 dc, ch 2, 2 dc) in next ch 1 space, dc in next st, **ch 2, sk next 2 sts, sc in next st, ch 2, skip next 2 sts, dc in next st*, rep from **

once, rep between * and * twice, (2 dc, ch 2, 2 dc) in next ch 1 space, dc in next st, ch 2, sk next 2 sts, sc in next st, ch 2, skip next 2 sts, join with sl st in top of beg ch 3. (28 dc, 8 sc)

Round 6: ch 3, dc in each of next 2 sts, *(2 dc, ch 2, 2 dc) in next ch 2 space, dc in each of next 3 sts, 2 dc in next ch 2 sp, dc in next st, ch 1, skip next ch 2 sp, sc in next st, ch 1, skip next ch 2 sp, dc in next st, 2 dc in next ch 2 sp, dc in each of next 3 sts, rep from * twice, *(2 dc, ch 2, 2 dc) in next ch 2 space, dc in each of next 3 sts, 2 dc in next ch 2 sp, dc in next st, ch 1, skip next ch 2 sp, sc in next st, ch 1, skip next ch 2 sp, dc in next st, 2 dc in next ch 2 sp, join with sl st in top of beg ch 3. (64 dc, 4 sc)

Round 7: ch 3, dc in each of next 4 sts, *(2 dc, ch 2, 2 dc) in next ch 2 space, dc in each of next 8 sts, 2 dc in next ch 1 sp, dc in next st, 2 dc in next ch 1 sp, dc in each of next 8 sts, rep from * twice, *(2 dc, ch 2, 2 dc) in next ch 2 space, dc in each of next 8 sts, 2 dc in next ch 1 sp, dc in next st, 2 dc in next ch 1 sp, dc in each of next 3 sts, join with sl st in top of beg ch 3. (100 dc)

Round 8: ch 1, sc in same st, (ch 3, skip next 2 sts, sc in next st) twice, *(sc, ch 2, sc) in next ch 2 sp, sc in next st, (ch 3, skip next 2 sts, sc in next st) 8 times, rep from * twice, (sc, ch 2, sc) in next ch 2 sp, sc in next st, (ch 3, skip next 2 sts, sc in next st) 5 times, ch 2, join with sl st in top of beg sc. (24 ch 3 sps)

Round 9: sl st into next ch 3 sp, ch 3, 2 dc in same space, sk next sc, 3 dc in next ch 3 sp, *sk next sc, dc in next st, (2 dc, ch 2, 2 dc) in next ch 2 sp, dc in next st, sk next st, (3 dc in next ch 3 sp) 8 times, rep from * twice more, sk next sc, dc in next st, (2 dc, ch 2, 2 dc) in next ch 2 sp, dc in next st, sk next st, (3 dc in next ch 3 sp) 6 times, join with sl st in top of beg ch 3. (120 dc)

Round 10: make beg cluster, (ch 2, make cluster) twice, ch 1, (2 dc, ch 2, 2 dc) in next ch 2 sp, *ch 1, (make cluster, ch 2) 9 times, make cluster, ch 1, (2 dc, ch 2, 2 dc) in next ch 2 sp, rep from * twice more, ch 1, (make cluster, ch 2) 8 times, join with sl st in top of beg cluster. (40 clusters)

Round 11: sl st in next ch 2 sp, ch 2, 2 hdc in same sp, (sk next cluster st, 3 hdc in next ch sp) twice, *sk next st, hdc in next st, (hdc, ch 2, hdc) in next ch sp, hdc in next st, sk next st, 3 hdc in next ch sp, (sk next cluster st, 3 hdc in next ch sp) 10 times, rep from * twice, sk next st, hdc in next st, (hdc, ch 2, hdc) in next ch sp, hdc in next st, sk next st, 3 hdc in next ch sp, (sk next cluster st, 3 hdc in next ch sp) 7 times, join with sl st in top of be ch 2, fasten off, weave in ends. (148 hdc)

****

<u>Wrist Warmers</u>

Step 1

Make a slip knot on your hook, and chain 30. Use your 5mm hook to do this, which ensures the chain won't be too tight later.

Step 2

Join into the first chain, being careful not to twist the chain. Use your 4mm hook from now on. The chain should now fit your wrist. If it's too tight, add a few stitches; if it's too big, make your chain a few stitches smaller.

Step 3

Chain 2, and work 1hdc in each stitch around. You now have 30 stitches. Join with a slip stitch to the top chain of your beginning chain 2.

Step 4

Work one more round of hdc stitches around (30). For the next two rows, work your hdc stitches into the back loops only. This gives your piece a little ridge in each row, which makes for an interesting texture. You now have 4 rows of hdc, of which the last two are done into the back loops.

Step 5

Change color. Work 2 rows of hdc around.

Step 6

Work 2 more rows of hdc around, but work your stitches into the back loops only.

Step 7

Change color. Work 2 rows of hdc around.

Step 8

Work 2 more rows of hdc around, but work your stitches into the back loops only.

Step 9

Change color. Work 1 row of hdc. For the second row, chain 2, work 11 hdc stitches, then chain 8, skip 8 stitches, then continue to hdc until the end of the row. This creates the thumb hole.

Step 10

Work 2 rows of hdc into the back loops only. Be sure to work 8 stitches into the thumb hole chain. The total count of stitches should be 30.

Step 11

Change color. Work 2 rows of hdc around.

Step 12

Work 2 rows of hdc into the back loops only.

2. Crochet the Edging

Don't cut the yarn. After joining the round: chain 1, work 1sc into the same stitch, ch 1, then *sc, ch1* around. This creates a nice frilly edging to gives your wrist warmers a finished look. Cut the yarn and sew in the ends.

Attach your yarn to the bottom of your wrist warmer, and crochet the same edging.

****

<u>Mountain Ridges Afghan 12 " Square</u>

Ch 38

Step 1: dc in 4ht ch from hook, dc across

Step 2: ch 3, fp tr in next 5, dc next 6. * fp tr next 6, dc next 6 *, repeat from * to * across, turn work

Step 3: ch 3, dc next 4, bp tr next 6 * dc next 6, bp tr next 6 *, repeat from * to * across, dc in beg ch 3, turn work

Step 4: ch 3, dc next st, fp tr next 6, * dc next 6, fp tr next 6 *, repeat from * to * across, dc in beg ch 3, turn work

Step 5: ch 3, dc next 2, bp tr next 6, * dc next 6, bp tr next 6 *, repeat from * to * across, dc next 2, dc in beg ch 3, turn work

Step 6: ch 3, dc next 3, fp tr next 6, * dc next 6, fp tr next 6 *, repeat from * to * across, dc next st dc in beg ch 3, turn work

Step 7: ch 3, bp tr next 6, * dc next 6, bp tr next 6 *, repeat from * to * across, dc next 4, dc in beg ch 3, turn work

Step 8: ch 3, dc next 5, * fp tr next 6, dc next 6 *, repeat from * to * across, fp tr next 6, dc in beg ch 3, turn work

Step 9: ch 3, bp tr next 4, dc next 6, * bp tr next 6, dc next 6 *, repeat from * to * across, dc in beg ch 3, turn work

Step 10: ch 3, fp tr next 6, dc next 6 * fp tr next 6, dc next 6 *, repeat from * to * across, fp tr next 3, dc in beg ch 3, turn work

Step 11: ch 3, bp tr next 2, dc next 6, * bp tr next 6, dc next 6 *, repeat from * to * across, bp tr next 2, dc in beg ch 3, turn work

Step 12: ch 3, fp tr next 3, dc next 6, * fp tr next 6, dc next 6 *, repeat from * to * across, fp tr next 2, dc in beg ch 3, turn work

Step 13: ch 3, * dc next 6, bp tr next 6 *, repeat from * to * across, bp tr next 4, dc in beg ch 3

Steps 14-20: repeat rows 2-8. 12 inch square, you can continue rows until desired length is reached, however it will no longer be a square.

****

Luxury Scarf

Very simple pattern

Ch 34

Row 1: sc in 2nd ch from hook, sc across to end, turn work

Row 2: ch 2, skip 1st st, dc across to end, turn work

Row 3: ch 1, sc across to end, turn work

Row 2 and 3 make pattern,

Row 4-133 repeat rows 2-3.

You can add a border or fringe to the ends if you would like.

****

<u>Amigurumi Crochet Cow</u>

- sc – single crochet
  - ch – chain

- sc2inc – two single crochets in one stitch (single crochet increase)
- sc2tog – single crochet two stitches together (single crochet decrease)
- sl st – slip stitch
- ML – magic loop, also known as magic ring or magic circle.

Let's start!

The Body – from the bottom (use 3mm hook)

- Cow is about 6 inches tall
-
  - 1. sc6 in ML   (6)
  - 2. sc2inc x 6   (12)
  - 3. (sc, sc2inc) x 6   (18)
  - 4. (sc2, sc2inc) x 6   (24)
  - 5. (sc3, sc2inc) x 6   (30)
  - 6. (sc4, sc2inc) x 6   (36)
  - 7. (sc11, sc2inc) x 3   (39)
  - 8. – 15. sc39 around   (39)
  - 16. (sc11, sc2tog) x 3   (36)
  - 17. (sc10, sc2tog) x 3   (33)
  - 18. (sc9, sc2tog) x 3   (30)

- 19. (sc8, sc2tog) x 3   (27)
- 20. (sc7, sc2tog) x 3   (24)
- 21. (sc6, sc2tog) x 3   (21)
- 22. (sc5, sc2tog) x 3   (18)

Slip stitch, fasten off and leave a long tale for sewing. Stuff the body.

The Head – work in oval

- 1. ch4 (4)
- 2. in 2nd chain from hook sc2inc, sc, sc3inc, sc1, sc1 in the same chain you did sc2inc   (8)
- 3. sc3inc (in the first stitch of sc2inc you made in 2nd row), sc3, sc3inc, sc3   (12)
- 4. sc2inc, sc, sc2inc, sc3, sc2inc, sc, sc2inc, sc3   (16)
- 5. sc2inc, sc3, sc2inc, sc3, sc2inc, sc3, sc2inc, sc3   (20)
- 6. sc2inc, sc5, sc2inc, sc3, sc2inc, sc5, sc2inc, sc3   (24)
- 7. sc2inc, sc7, sc2inc, sc3, sc2inc, sc7, sc2inc, sc3   (28)
- 8. sc, sc2inc, sc7, sc2inc, sc5, sc2inc, sc7, sc2inc, sc4   (32)
- 9. sc2, sc2inc, sc7, sc2inc, sc7, sc2inc, sc7, sc2inc, sc5   (36)
- 10. sc3, sc2inc, sc3, sc2inc, sc3, sc2inc, sc9, sc2inc, sc3, sc2inc, sc3, sc2inc, sc6   (42)

77

- *11. – 20. sc42 around   (42)*
- *21. (sc5, sc2tog) x 6   (36)*
- *22. (sc4, sc2tog) x 6   (30)*
- *23. (sc3, sc2tog) x 6   (24)*
- *24. (sc2, sc2tog) x 6   (18)*

Now is a good time to place the safety eyes. Between rows 11 and 12, 6 stitches apart. You can stuff the head now.

- *25. (sc, sc2tog) x 6   (12)*
- *26. sc2tog x 6   (6)*

Close the head, and fasten off. Sew the head onto the body.

The Nose – work in oval

- *1. ch8   (8)*
- *2. in 2nd chain from hook sc2inc, sc5, sc3inc, sc5, sc1 in the same chain you did sc2inc (16)*
- *3. sc3inc (in the first stitch of sc2inc you made in 2nd row), sc7, sc3inc, sc7   (20)*
- *4. (sc2inc, sc, sc2inc, sc7) x 2*
                        (24)

78

- 5. (sc2inc, sc3, sc2inc, sc7) x 2

  (28)
- 6. (sc2inc, sc5, sc2inc, sc7) x 2

  (32)
- 7. (sc2inc, sc7, sc2inc, sc7) x 2

  (36)
- 8. sc, sc2inc, sc7, sc2inc, sc9, sc2inc, sc7, sc2inc, sc8   (40)

Slip stitch, and fasten off. Leave a long tail for sewing. Sew the nose onto the head, but put some stuffing before you close it entirely.

The Legs – make two

- 1. sc6 in ML   (6)
- 2. sc2inc x 6   (12)
- 3. (sc, sc2inc) x 6   (18)
- 4. sc18 in back loop only   (18)
- 5. sc18 in both loops   (18)

Use a different color.

- 6. – 10. sc18 around   (18)
- 11. (sc4, sc2tog) x 3   (15)

- 12. (sc3, sc2tog) x 3   (12)
- 13. (sc2, sc2tog) x 3   (9) — putt some stuffing on the bottom.
- 14. (sc, sc2tog) x 3   (6)
- 15. sc6 around   (6)

Close it, and fasten off. Leave a long tail for sewing. Make two legs.

The Front Legs — make two

- 1. sc6 in ML   (6)
- 2. sc2inc x 6   (12)
- 3. sc12 in back loop only   (12)
- 4. sc12 in both loops   (12)

Use a different color.

- 5. – 9. sc12 around   (12)
- 10. (sc2, sc2tog) x 3   (9) — putt some stuffing on the bottom.
- 11. (sc, sc2tog) x 3   (6)
- 12. sc6 around   (6)

Close it, and fasten off. Leave a long tail for sewing.

****

Amigurumi Misfit Mermaid

Ch 1 is not considered the first sc, to join each round sl st into the first sc, skipping over the ch 1

- Unless otherwise noted, each decrease (sc2tog) will be placed in the back, in the last set of sts (arms and tail).
- All rounds of body are joined, rounds in arms and part of the tail are not joined and are made in a spiral, use stitch markers
  - The pattern will specify times to add poly fill
- Hair is attached in the same manner as you would attach fringe to any project, for best results do not make each strand the same exact length and attach asymmetrically

STITCHES USED

sc – single crochet, sl st – slip stitch, blo – back loop only, hdc – half double crochet, dc – double crochet, tr – treble crochet

sc2tog– single crochet two together insert hook into first st, yarn over and pull through st (two loops on hook), insert hook into the next st, yarn over and pull through st (three loops on hook), yarn over and pull through all three loops on hook

Round 1: Beginning with main color Ch 2, 8sc in first chain, sl st into first sc to join into ring <8>

Round 2: 2sc in each st around <16>

Round 3: *Sc in next st, 2sc in next st, repeat from * around <24>

Round 4: Sc in each st around <24>

Round 5: *Sc in next 2sts, 2sc in next st, repeat from * around <32>

Round 6: Sc in each st around <32>

Round 7: *Sc in next 3sts, 2sc in next st, repeat from * around <40>

Rounds 8-14: Sc in each st around <40>

Round 15: *Sc in next 3sts, sc2tog, repeat from * around <32>

Round 16: Sc in each st around <32>

Round 17: *Sc in next 2sts, sc2tog, repeat from * around <24>

Round 18: *Sc next st, sc2tog, repeat from * around <16>

Fill

Rounds 19-20: Sc in each st around <16>

Round 21: 2sc in each st around <32>

Rounds 22-24: Sc in each st around <32>

Rounds 25: Sc in next 4 sts, [ch 4, skip 4sts], sc in next 11sts, [ch 4, skip 4sts], sc in remaining 9 sts

Round 26: Sc in next 4sts (place st marker in last st), *sc in blo of next 4chs **, sc next 11 sts (place st marker in first and last st), repeat from * to **, sc in remaining 9sts (place st marker in first st). Pull up long loop and cut main color, do not sl st to join (you will join round when joining next color for fin section)

ARMS— arms are made in a spiral and rounds are not joined, mark first st of each round to keep row count

Round 1: Attach yarn by sl st into any st of opening just made (preferably in the back), sc in each st and in marked sts <10>

Rounds 2-6: Sc in each st around <10>

Rounds 7-10: Sc in each st around, to last 2sts, sc2tog <each row will decrease by one st, round 10 will be 6sts> pull yarn on hook through the loop, using yarn needle weave tail out through next st and in through next st around, pull tight, secure, fasten and push needle through to inside of arm, anchor st to secure and fasten off.

Repeat for other arm. Fill both arms

Bust and Tail— Change to fin color on sl st of final body round— fill as you go for entire section, ignore marked sts from when arms were made.

Round 1: Sc in next 10sts, *hdc in one row above, [dc in two rows above]2x, hdc in one row above**, sc in next st, repeat from * to **, sc in remaining 13sts <32>

Rounds 2-3: Sc in next 10 sts, *hdc one row above in next 4 sts**, sc in next st, repeat from * to **, sc in remaining 13sts <32>

FROM NOW TO END— you will be working in spirals, spiral rounds are not joined, mark first st of each round to keep row count

Rounds 4-7: Sc in each st around <32>

Rounds 8-15: Sc in each st till two sts remain, sc2tog <each round will decrease by one st, 24sc at the end of round 15>

Rounds 16-17: Sc in each st around <24>

Be sure Tail is completely stuffed

Round 18: *sc in next st, sc2tog, repeat from * around <16>

Round 19: *sc next 2sts, sc2tog, repeat from * around <12>

Round 20: *sc next st, sc2tog, repeat from * around <8>

Fill last 3 rounds as needed

Fin – depending on how your spirals worked out on the tail. You will want to have 4sc sts in front and 4sc stitches in back with the ch10 on each side.

Round 1: *Sc in the next 4sts, ch 11, sc back down the chain <10>, repeat from *

Round 2: Sc2tog 2x, **working up the ch10, sc in next 2sts, hdc in next st, dc in next 2sts, 2tr in next st, dc in the next 2sts, hdc in the next st, sc in the next st, ch 2 at the top of the ch10 and sl st into the first ch just made, working back down the ch10, sc in the first st, hdc in the next st, dc in next 2sts, 2tr in the next st, dc in next 2sts, hdc in next st, sc in next 2sts, sc2tog 2x on round and repeat from **

FINISHING

Pull yarn through loop on hook, attach needle, going from back to front insert hook in first st and coordinating st on front, going from back to front insert hook in next st and corresponding st on back.

Working with back of mermaid facing, head down, *from back to front, insert hook on first st on inside of fin and going from front to back insert hook in first st on inside second fin. Repeat from * for second and third inside sts on fins

****

Amigurumi Tree Frog

Head & Body
1: ch 7, sc in 2n ch from hook, sc 5 = [6]
2: (* sc 1st st , 2 sc next *, repeat x 3 = [9]
3: sc 2, inc3, sc 3, inc3, sc 2 = [13]

4: sc 3, inc3, sc 5, inc3, sc 3 = [17]

5: sc 6, inc, sc, inc, sc, inc, sc 6 = [20]

Place a stitch marker between the 12th and 13th stitch on round 6 and leave it there. This marks the center of the forehead. Use it as guide when placing the eyes.

6: sc 5, inc3, sc 9, inc3, sc 4 = [24]

7-9: sc in each stitch = [24]

Attach safety eyes to either side of the stitch marker, between rows 6 and 7, leaving 8 stitches (count 7 holes) between them.

10: sc 8, dec, (sc, dec) x 3, sc 5 = [20]

Start stuffing the head. Keep adding a bit of fiberfill after every few rounds, stuffing the head and body firmly.

11: sc 7, inc, (sc, inc) x 4, sc 4 = [25]

12: sc 7, inc, sc 12, inc, sc 4 = [27]

13-16: sc in each stitch = [27]

17: sc 6, dec x 2, sc 5, dec, sc 4, dec x 2, sc 2 = [22]

18: sc 6, dec x 2, sc 2, dec, sc 2, dec x 2, sc 2 = [17]

19: sc 5, dec x 2, sc, dec, sc, dec x 2 = [12]

20: dec x 6 = [6]

Finish stuffing. Cut the yarn, leaving a long yarn tail

Front legs (make 2)

1: ch 6, sc 5 = [5]

2-14: sc in each stitch = [5]

Cut the yarn, leaving a long yarn tail for sewing. Do not stuff the legs.

Back legs (make 2)

1: ch 6, sc 5 = [5]

2-17: sc in each stitch = [5]

Cut the yarn, leaving a long yarn tail for sewing, Do not stuff the legs.

Cut two pieces of wire long enough to fit inside the legs and through the body, plus about 5 cm (2") so you can bend back the ends. Push the wires through the body where you want the legs to be.

Bend the end back and then wrap a bit of tape around the wire end to make sure it won't poke through the fabric.

Push the wire inside the leg and sew it to the body.

Hold up the other leg and bend the wire so it's the right length. Push it inside the second leg and sew the leg to the body. Do the same with the front legs.

Bend the legs to shape.

Toes (make 8)

1: ch 5, sc 4 = [4]

2-3: sc in each stitch = [4]

Cut the yarn, leaving a long yarn tail for sewing. Do not stuff the toes.

Sew the toes to the legs. Fasten and hide all yarn tails.

*****

<u>Pencil Holder</u>

Pencil tube

1: ch 2, 6 sc in 2nd ch from hook, sl st close.

2: 1 sc, 2 sc, repeat around, sl st close.

3: 1 sc, 2 sc, repeat around, sl st close, finish off.

4: attach new color..... 1 sc, 2 sc in next st, sc next 3, 2 sc in next st, sc next 4, 2 sc next st, sl st close, finish off.

5: attach new color..... sc next 5, 2 sc next st, repeat around, sl st close

6: sc back loop around

7-30: sc around. Sl st close finish off.

Pencil point

1. ch 2, 6 sc in 2nd ch from hook

2. ch 1, *sc next , 2 sc in next* repeat around from * to *

3. ch 1, sc around

4. ch 1, * sc next 2, 2 sc in next* repeat around from * to *

5. ch 1, * sc next 3, 2 sc in next* repeat around from * to *

6. ch 1, sc next 4, 2 sc in next* repeat around from * to * sl st close finish off.

7. add new color:

89

sc in any sc from previous row * sc next 5, 2 sc in next* repeat around from * to *

8. ch 1, sc next 6, 2 sc in next* repeat around from * to *

9. ch 1, sc next 7, 2 sc in next* repeat around from * to *

10. ch 1, sc next 8, 2 sc in next* repeat around from * to *

11. sc around

12. ch 1, sc next 9, 2 sc in next* repeat around from * to *

13. ch 1, sc next 10, 2 sc in next* repeat around from * to *

14. ch 1, sc next 11, 2 sc in next* repeat around from * to *

15. sc around

16. ch 1, sc next 12, 2 sc in next* repeat around from * to *

17-19. sc around, sl st close, finish off.

Attached to pencil tube, sc 4 st.

One Hour Slippers

children pattern, for young adult and adult use a bigger hook and repeat round 4, 5 times then proceed to round 6

Material: 4 mm crochet hook

Yarn needle

Scissors

1} Chain 3. sl st in 1st st to form circle. DC 6 times in loop, sl st close.

2} Ch 3, 2 dc in each st around. sl st to close.

3} Ch 3, dc in same st, * 2dc in next, dc next st *. repeat from * to * around. sl st to close.

4} Ch 3, dc each st around, sl st to close.

5} Repeat 4

6} Ch 3, dc next 20, ch 3 turn

7-8} Repeat 6

Cut yard leaving about 5 inches to sew ends together.

Turn inside out, fold flat ends together and sl st or whip st.

****

****

****

Summer air tunic

Material: 3.5 mm crochet hook

Yarn needle

Scissors

Abbreviations

Note: I used chainless starting dc for every first dc of each row/ round instead of ch 3. There's another good crochet technique to use is ch 2, dc into same stitch (counted as 1st dc). In the pattern below you'll see I simply state dc into 1st stitch for every first dc of each row/round, so just choose your best technique

Special stitches used:

2dc-V stitch: (2dc, ch1, 2dc) into same stitch or space.

This crochet Summer air tunic pattern fits size L (chest size 36 to 38 inches)

Skill level: Intermediate

Gauge: 10 double crochet stitches x 4 rows approximately 2 inches (with materials indicated)

Back:

R1: ch 117, dc into 3rd ch from hook (first 2 ch doesn't count as 1st dc), 115 dc across, turn.

R2: *dc, skip 2 sts, 2dc-V stitch into next st, skip 2 sts, dc into next st, ch2, skip 2 sts* repeat ** 12 times across, dc into next st, skip 2 sts, 2dc-V stitch into next st, skip 2 sts, dc into last st, turn.

R3: *dc, skip 2 sts, 2dc-V stitch into next ch1-space, skip 2 sts, dc into next st, ch 2, skip next ch2-space* repeat ** 12 times across, dc into next st, skip 2 sts, 2dc-V stitch into next ch1-space, skip 2 sts, dc into last st, turn.

R4 to R58: same as R3

R59: *dc, skip 2 sts, 2dc-V stitch into next ch1-space, skip 2 sts, dc into next st, ch 2, skip next ch2-space* repeat ** 4 times across, dc into next st, turn.

R60: *dc, ch2, skip next ch2-space, dc into next st, skip 2 sts, 2dc-V stitch into next ch1-space, skip 2 sts* repeat ** 4 times across, dc into last st. (fasten off, leave long end for shoulder seaming)

Repeat R59 and R60 at the other side.

Front:

R1: ch 117, dc into 3rd ch from hook (first 2 ch doesn't count as 1st dc), 115 dc across, turn.

R2: *dc, skip 2 sts, 2dc-V stitch into next st, skip 2 sts, dc into next st, ch2, skip 2 sts* repeat ** 12 times across, dc into next st, skip 2 sts, 2dc-V stitch into next st, skip 2 sts, dc into last st, turn.

R3: *dc, skip 2 sts, 2dc-V stitch into next ch1-space, skip 2 sts, dc into next st, ch 2, skip next ch2-space* repeat ** 12 times across, dc into next st, skip 2 sts, 2dc-V stitch into next ch1-space, skip 2 sts, dc into last st, turn.

R4 to R55: same as R3

R56: *dc, skip 2 sts, 2dc-V stitch into next ch1-space, skip 2 sts, dc into

94

next st, ch 2, skip next ch2-space* repeat ** 4 times across, dc into next st, turn.

R57: *dc, ch2, skip next ch2-space, dc into next st, skip 2 sts, 2dc-V stitch into next ch1-space, skip 2 sts* repeat ** 4 times across, dc into last st, turn.

R58: *dc, skip 2 sts, 2dc-V stitch into next ch1-space, skip 2 sts, dc into next st, ch 2, skip next ch2-space* repeat ** 4 times across, dc into last st, turn.

R59: same as R57

R60: same as R58 (fasten off, leave long end for shoulder seaming)

Repeat R56 and R60 at the other side.

Seam shoulder lines with sc.

Seam body lines with sc. (leave 18 rows from the top down for armholes, leave 12 to 15 rows for side slits)

****

****

****

Pineapple racerback tank top

Materials: 5mm crochet hook

Yarn needle

Scissors

Abbreviations

Note: I used chainless starting dc for every first dc of each round instead of ch 3. There's another good crochet technique to use is ch 2, dc into same stitch (counted as 1st dc). In the pattern below you'll see I simply state dc into 1st stitch for every first dc of each round, so just choose your best technique

Special stitch used: 2dc-V stitch (2 dc, ch 2, 2 dc into same stitch or space)

This crochet pineapple racerback tank top pattern fits size L (chest size: 36

to 38 inches)

Gauge: 5 double crochet stitches approximately 1.5 inches after steam blocking (with materials indicated)

Top: (crochet in rounds)

Ch 114, sl into 1st stitch to join.

R1: dc around, 114 sts, sl into 1st stitch to join.

R2: *dc, skip 2 sts, 2dc-V stitch into next st, ch 3, skip 3 sts, sc into next st, ch 6, skip 3 sts, sc into next st, ch 3, skip 3 sts, 2dc-V stitch into next st, skip 2 sts, dc into next st * repeat ** 6 times around, sl into 1st stitch to join.

R3: *dc, 2dc-V stitch into next ch2-space, 9 tr into next ch6-space, 2dc-V stitch into next ch2-space, dc into next st* repeat ** 6 times around, sl into 1st stitch to join.

R4: *dc, 2dc-V stitch into next ch2-space, ch 2, sc into next st (the tr of previous round), (ch 3, skip 1 st, sc into next st) x 4 times, ch 2, 2dc-V stitch into next ch2-space, dc into next st* repeat ** 6 times around, sl into

1st stitch to join.

R5: *dc, 2dc-V stitch into next ch2-space, ch 3, sc into next ch3-space, (ch 3, sc into next ch3-space) x 3 times, ch 3, 2dc-V stitch into next ch2-space, dc into next st* repeat ** 6 times around, sl into 1st stitch to join.

R6: *dc, 2dc-V stitch into next ch2-space, ch 4, sc into next ch3-space, (ch 3, sc into next ch3-space) x 2 times, ch 4, 2dc-V stitch into next ch2-space, dc into next st* repeat ** 6 times around, sl into 1st stitch to join.

R7: *dc, 2dc-V stitch into next ch2-space, ch 5, sc into next ch3-space, ch 3, sc into next ch3-space, ch 5, 2dc-V stitch into next ch2-space, dc into next st* repeat ** 6 times around, sl into 1st stitch to join.

R8: *dc, 2dc-V stitch into next ch2-space, ch 8, sc into next ch3-space, ch 8, 2dc-V stitch into next ch2-space, dc into next st* repeat ** 6 times around, sl into 1st stitch to join.

R9: *dc, 2dc-V stitch into next ch2-space, ch 3, sc into next ch8-space, ch 6, sc into next ch8-space, ch 3, 2dc-V stitch into next ch2-space, dc into next st* repeat ** 6 times around, sl into 1st stitch to join.

R10: same as R3.

R11: same as R4

R12: same as R5

R13: same as R6

R14: same as R7

R15: same as R8

R16: same as R9

Repeat (R10 to R16) x 2 times. Until you reach R30

R31: same as R3

R32: ch1, hdc around, sl into 1st stitch to join. (fasten off, weave in end)

Back part and shoulder straps:

Back part:

R1: From the 1st ch of 114 chain, sc around, total 114 sts, sl into 1st stitch to join (fasten off, weave in end)

R2: From the 1st stitch of R1, skip 15 sts, crochet 27 sc across, total 27 sts.

R3: turn, 5 dc across, skip 2 sts, 2dc-V stitch into next st, ch 3, skip 3 sts, sc into next st, ch 6, skip 3 sts, sc into next st, ch 3, skip 3 sts, 2dc-V stitch into next st, skip 2 sts, 5 dc across.

R4: turn, 5 dc across, skip 2 sts, 2dc-V stitch into next ch2-space, 9 tr into next ch6-space, 2dc-V stitch into next ch2-space, 5 dc across.

R5: turn, 5 dc across, 2dc-V stitch into next ch2-space, ch 2, sc into next st, (ch 3, skip 1 st, sc into next st) x 4 times, ch 2, 2dc-V stitch into next ch2-space, 5 dc across.

R6: turn, 5 dc across, 2dc-V stitch into next ch2-space, ch 3, sc into next ch3-space, (ch 3, sc into next ch3-space) x 3 times, ch 3, 2dc-V stitch into next ch2-space, 5 dc across.

R7: turn, 5 dc across, 2dc-V stitch into next ch2-space, ch 4, sc into next ch3-space, (ch 3, sc into next ch3-space) x 2 times, ch 4, 2dc-V stitch into next ch2-space, 5 dc across.

R8: turn, 5 dc across, 2dc-V stitch into next ch2-space, ch 5, sc into next ch3-space, ch 3, sc into next ch3-space, ch 5, 2dc-V stitch into next ch2-space, 5 dc across.

R9: turn, 5 dc across, 2dc-V stitch into next ch2-space, ch 6, sc into next ch3-space, ch 6, 2dc-V stitch into next ch2-space, 5 dc across.

****
****

Crochet Pineapple Tunic

Materials: 3.25 mm crochet hook

Yarn needle

Scissors

2dc-V stitch: (2 dc, ch 2, 2 dc) into same stitch or space

Front: work in rows

R1: Ch 78, dc into 3rd ch from hook, (the first 2 ch doesn't count as 1st dc), skip 2 ch, 2dc – V stitch into next ch, ch3, skip 3ch, sc into next ch, ch6, skip 3ch, sc into next ch, ch3, skip 3ch, 2dc-V stitch into next ch, skip 2ch, dc into next ch,* dc into next ch, skip 2ch, 2dc-V stitch into next ch, ch3, skip 3ch, sc into next ch, ch6, skip 3ch, sc into next ch, ch3, skip 3ch, 2dc- V stitch into next ch, skip 2ch, dc into next ch* repeat ** 3 times.

R2: turn, * dc, 2dc-V stitch into next ch2-space, 9 tr into ch6-space, 2dc-V stitch into next ch2-space, dc into next st* repeat ** 4 times.

R3: turn, * dc, 2dc- V stitch into next ch2-space, ch2, sc into next st, (ch3, skip 1 st, sc into next st) x 4 times, ch2, 2dc-V stitch into next ch2-space, dc into next st* repeat ** 4 times.

R4: turn, * dc, 2dc- V stitch into next ch2-space, ch3, sc into next ch3-space, (ch3, sc into next space) x 3 times, ch3, 2dc-V stitch into next ch2-space, dc into next st* repeat ** 4 times.

R5: turn, * dc, 2dc- V stitch into next ch2-space, ch4, sc into next ch3-space, (ch3, sc into next space) x 2 times, ch4, 2dc-V stitch into next ch2-space, dc into next st* repeat ** 4 times.

R6: turn, * dc, 2dc- V stitch into next ch2-space, ch5, sc into next ch3-space, ch3, sc into next space, ch5, 2dc-V stitch into next ch2-space, dc into next st* repeat ** 4 times.

R7: turn, * dc, 2dc- V stitch into next ch2-space, ch8, sc into ch3-space, ch8, 2dc-V stitch into next ch2-space, dc into next st* repeat ** 4 times.

R8: turn, * dc, 2dc-V stitch into next ch2-space, ch3, sc into ch8-space, ch6, sc into next ch8-space, ch3, 2dc- V stitch into next ch2-space, dc into next st * repeat ** 4 times.

R9: same as R2

R10: same as R3

R11: same as R4

R12: same as R5

R13: same as R6

R14: same as R7

Repeat (from R8 to R14) x 7 more times, until you reach R56 (fasten off)

Shoulder part: back to R1 of the front.

R1: insert hook into the 1st ch of R1, dc into 1st ch, skip 2ch, 2dc-V stitch into next ch, ch3, skip 3ch, sc into next ch, ch6, skip 3ch, sc into next ch, ch3, skip 3ch, 2dc- V stitch into next ch, skip 2ch, dc into next ch.

R2: turn, dc, 2dc- V stitch into next ch2-space, 9 tr into ch6-space, 2dc-V stitch into next ch2-space, dc into last st.

R3: turn, dc, 2dc- V stitch into next ch2-space, ch2, sc into next st, (ch3, skip 1 st, sc into next st) x 4 times, ch2, 2dc- V stitch into next ch2-space, dc into last st.

R4: turn, dc, 2dc- V stitch into next ch2-space, ch3, sc into next ch3-space, (ch3, sc into next space) x 3 times, ch3, 2dc-V stitch into next ch2-space, dc into last st.

R5: turn, dc, 2dc- V stitch into next ch2-space, ch4, sc into next ch3-space, (ch3, sc into next space) x 2 times, ch4, 2dc-V stitch into next ch2-space, dc into last st.

R6: turn, dc, 2dc- V stitch into next ch2-space, ch5, sc into next ch3-space, ch3, sc into next space, ch5, 2dc-V stitch into next ch2-space, dc into last st.

R7: turn, dc, 2dc- V stitch into next ch2-space, ch8, sc into ch3-space, ch8, 2dc-V stitch into next ch2-space, dc into last st (fasten off, leave long end for seaming)

Repeat at other side to make the other one.

Back: work in rows

From R1 to R14: same as front part

Repeat (from R8 to R14) x 8 times until you reach R63.

Shoulder part: back to R1 of the back.

R1: insert hook into the 1st ch of R1, dc into 1st ch, skip 2ch, 2dc-V stitch into next ch, ch3, skip 3ch, sc into next ch, ch6, skip 3ch, sc into next ch, ch3, skip 3ch, 2dc- V stitch into next ch, skip 2ch, dc into next ch.

R2: turn, dc, 2dc- V stitch into next ch2-space, 9 tr into ch6-space, 2dc-V stitch into next ch2-space, dc into last st (fasten off, leave long end for seaming)

Repeat at other side to make the other one.

From the wrong side, seam shoulder parts with sc or sl (cluster of stitches: dc, 2dc-V stitch) at both sides of the shoulder part.

****

****

Cross Over table place mat

Materials: 4.25 mm crochet hook

Yarn needle

Scissors

1} Ch 57, sc in 2nd ch from hook and in each st across.

2} Ch 2, dc in same st, sk 1 st, dc in next, dc st that you just skipped to form cross over st.

Repeat row 2 until mat is desired length.

****

****

****

Spiral Scrubby

1} Ch 21, 2 sc in 2nd ch from hook. sc next 17, sc dec last 2.

2} working in back loop: Ch 1, sc 1st 2 tog, sc across, 2 sc in last st.

3} working in back loop: Ch 1, 2 sc in 1st st, sc cross, sc last 2 tog.

Repeat row 2 and 3 for 21 rows.

****

****

Arch Stitch Scarf

1} Ch 14. {dc, ch 3, dc} in 4th ch from hook. * ch 3, sk 3, sc next 3. Ch 3, sk 3, {dc, ch 3, dc} in next st * repeat from * to * to end of row

2} Ch 3, * 7 dc in ch 3 sp, ch 3, sc in middle of 3 sc in previous row, ch 3 * repeat from * top * to end of row.

3} Ch 1, sk 1, sc next 6. * ch 5, sc next 7 * repeat from * to * to end of row.

4} Ch 6, sk 2, * sc next 3, { ch 3, dc, ch 3 } in ch 5 sp, ch 3 *, repeat from * to * to end of row.

5} Ch 6, sc in middle of 3sc from previous row, ch 3, 7dc in ch 3 sp. repeat row to end, ending with ch 3, 1 dc in 3rd ch of ch 6 of previous row.

6} Ch 5, * sc next 7, ch 5 * re3peat from * to * to end of row, ending with sc in the 3rd ch of ch 6 of previous row.

7} Ch 3, * {dc, ch 3, dc} in next sp, ch 3 sc top 3 st of arch * repeat form * to * to end of row, ending with {dc, ch 3, dc} in ch 5 sp.

Repeat rows 2-7 until scarf is desired length.

****
****

Fan and V st scarf

1} Ch 17. { dc, ch2, dc } in 6th ch from hook. * sk 3, { dc, ch 2, dc } in next ch * repeat from * to * to last 3, sk 2, dc in last st.

2} Ch 3, * 4 dc in ch 3 sp * repeat across, dc in last st.

3} Ch 4, dc in same, * {dc, ch 2, dc } in sp between the two sets of 4 dc's of previous row, repeat to end, dc, ch 1, dc in last sp.

4} Ch 3, 2 dc in ch 1 sp, * 4 dc in ch 2 sp * repeat across row, ending with 3 dc in ch 3 sp.

5} Ch 3, { dc, ch 2, dc } in sp between 4dc of previous row, repeat across, dc in last sp.

Repeat row's 2-5 until desired length is reached.

****
****

Window Scarf

1} Ch 12. sc in 2nd ch from hook. sc across/ ch 1 turn.

2} sc across. ch 1 turn.

3} sc across. ch 2 turn.

4} dc in 1st st. * ch 1, sk 1, dc next st. * repeat * to * across. ch 1 turn.

5} repeat row 4 until desired length is reached.